THE CRAFT GIN GUIDE

THE CRAFT GIN GUIDE

David T. Smith and Ella Carr

Duncan Petersen

2nd edition

23456789

Conceived, designed and produced by
Duncan Petersen Publishing Ltd,
G9, 80 Silverthorne Road, Battersea, SW8 3HE

Sales representation in the UK and Ireland by
Heartwood Publishing Ltd
40 Forester Road, Bath, BA2 6QE
Distibuted by Grantham Books Services, NG31 7XQ

Editor Natalie Beecroft
Contributors Ella Carr, Alexander Duncan, David T. Smith,
Will Plows, Eleanor Pyne
Cover and layout design Nicky Collings
Maps Map Creation Ltd
Layout Natalie Beecroft
Photo credits Many of the photos were supplied by the bars and distilleries and
have been reproduced with their permission. See page 224 for other photo credits.
Front cover image: © River Test Distillery
Back cover images: © Ballyvolane © Animal Spirits © Scilly Spirit ©
© Bermondsey Distillery © Pixel Spirits
Editorial director Andrew Duncan

A CIP catalogue record for this book is available from the British Library.

ISBN 978-1-7396684-0-2

DTP by Duncan Petersen Publishing Ltd
Printed in the EU by Fine Tone

Created with a small financial contribution from the distillers and bars featured.
Opening times and prices were correct when we went to press but we
recommend checking the website or social media pages before visiting.

Contents

GINTRODUCTION

This unique new guide to craft gin is the first to feature not just gin but the new and enjoyable pastime of 'gintourism' – visiting microdistilleries to learn about gin, taste gin and even to make your own personal distillation. A large and growing number of craft gin makers see it as part of their business to welcome visitors for instructive tours.

The Craft Gin Guide covers what we believe are the most interesting small-batch microdistilleries, and gin bars, across Britain and Ireland. London was traditionally the centre

Selecting botanicals at Caprelous, page 95.

of gin distilling in England, but now small distilleries are everywhere, in towns, cities, villages and miles off the beaten track in remote countryside. The guide has searched them out wherever they are, including Scotland and Ireland, which are given due space.

The focus is overwhelmingly on genuine small-batch producers, but we do include a few large operations.

Gin is defined as a spirit flavoured with juniper berries. The essential feature of craft gin is its use of multiple botanicals alongside juniper to create unique, often local flavours. Most gins include orris and angelica root to stop the flavours bleeding into each other, so we have omitted these from our 'key botanicals' lists. Several of the processes are done by hand, for example gathering and preparing the botanicals, and bottling and labelling. Another characteristic of craft gin is making it in small batches – as few as, say, 100 bottles. This guide does not apply rigid rules about numbers of bottles – we feature distillers as long as they are relatively small operators aiming to create unique local gins.

Since the craft gin renaissance got going around 2010, the thirst for all gin, whether mainstream or craft, has grown dramatically. However, gin hasn't always been so popular. This introduction explains why it once went out of

fashion, and of course tells the story of the gin renaissance of the past decade.

One the joys of this subject is picturing small gin makers in their tiny premises, many in kitchens, garages and sheds. We hope the many original photographs help bring this alive for you.

A brief history of gin

The word 'gin' derives from genever, Dutch for juniper. Variations of gin have been used in medicine as far back as 70 AD, when the first mention of a gin-like substance was recorded in an encyclopaedia of herbal medicine – a solution of juniper berries macerated in wine was recommended for chest ailments. Dutch physician Sylvius de Bouve is widely credited with creating the first batch of gin as we know it today, calling it genever, in the 1600s. However, genever probably existed as early as the 1500s.

Genever found its way to Britain from The Netherlands in the 17thC, during the Thirty Years' War. English soldiers had been supporting the Dutch revolt against the Catholic Philip of Spain and were given genever before battle to give them 'Dutch Courage.' It grew ever popular in Britain, largely due to William of Orange's heavy taxes and blockades on French wine and brandy. He introduced The Corn Laws (heavy taxes on imported food and grain), and tax breaks on spirits production in Britain, encouraging people to find a use for their surplus, subpar grain, and make their own spirits – genever became the logical choice as it's usually made with grain, not grape. Beer was also heavily taxed to fund the War of the Grand Alliance, making it about the same price as genever, so people wanted to try it.

Gin's notoriously bad reputation arose in the 1700s with the coronation of Queen Anne, who cancelled the 1638 charter giving The Worshipful Company of Distillers monopoly over spirit production within a 21-mile radius of London. This meant they weren't able to

68. Gin Lane. Engraving by William Hogarth (3d state. 1751).

Hogarth's *Gin Lane*.

GINTRODUCTION

regulate the quality of the spirits and hundreds of illegal distilleries opened. Genever appealed to the poor as, by this time, it was cheaper than beer and safer to drink than water, but that is not saying much. The produce of illegal distilleries was, by modern standards, toxic.

By the early 18thC 'genever' had been anglicized to 'gin', and half of the drinking establishments in London were bars or taverns, with more than ten million gallons of gin being produced. Over the decade following 1723, the death rate in London surpassed the birth rate, and gin played its part. People would add to gin substances like turpentine for a resinous, woody flavour, and sulphuric acid for a sweet and more intoxicating effect. Gin was blamed for low fertility rates, babies born with deformities, and mother's neglecting their children, earning it the name Mother's Ruin. One particular story about a mother strangling her child to death to sell her clothes for gin sparked outrage and pushed the government to make drastic changes. Following two unsuccessful acts, The Gin Act of 1736 was passed. This required distillers to hold a licence which cost £50 a year. It also allowed the public to buy a minimum of two gallons at a time, with a tax of £1 per gallon. The industry suffered and illegal production became difficult as informers were paid £5 to report them. Several more acts were implemented after this, which imposed higher taxes and removed licences from retailers so gin became scarce.

Selection criteria

We include bars/distilleries that offer at least one of the following:

- Customer experiences
- Local appeal
- A range of small-batch craft gins – for a definition see page 6

In the back section of the guide are other bars and distilleries that weren't right for the main section – see page 210

Gin today

On the 14th March 2009, Fairfax Hall and Sam Galsworthy launched Sipsmith, London's first traditional copper distillery since 1820, aiming to bring London Dry Gin back to its rightful birthplace. They have been credited with sparking a ginaissance, with the spirit gradually becoming one of the UK's most popular, second only to vodka. According to *The Independent*, before the Covid-19 pandemic around 73 million bottles of gin were sold per year, with sales doubling between 2016 and 2018. Waitrose spirit buyer, John Vine,

claimed it was the local and regional brands that were driving sales. With the rising popularity of craft spirits and beers, this doesn't come as much of a surprise – people want to know exactly where their products are coming from.

Some credit gin's success to the fact that it's quick and cheap to make – it doesn't need to be aged like whisky. While this may be true, there's another, rather more fascinating trend: the phenomena of Millennials and social media. Maybe it's just coincidence that Instagram was created around the same time the gin revolution took off, but could it be that Instagram had a hand in the spirit's success?

Millennials are, in marketing terms, a large target group. Nothing gets them keener than the prospect of posting a fabulous Insta of a beautiful tablescape and the likes rolling in. A beautifully-garnished gin on a millennial's Instagram is effectively free advertising for distilleries.

Gin is a versatile spirit – it must include juniper but, beyond that, distillers can experiment with different flavours. This has widened the market and made gins more varied and Instagrammable. As we went to press, there had been more than 10 million Instagram posts with #gin, and almost all of them were of colourful or shimmery drinks, gin cocktails, or G&Ts with bright flowers and fruit garnishes (see top left).

And it's not just the spirit itself that has been given a makeover. As you'll see in this guide, a growing number of gin bars are making themselves Instagrammable, tapping into the trend of flower walls (top right), and Shoreditch-style shabby-chic.

GIN JOURNEYS – LONDON

Gintourism is a great way to get to know a city. These are gin journeys you can follow in London, Edinburgh and Dublin.

Beefeater Gin Distillery to Mr Fogg's Gin Parlour

Begin with a tour of the Beefeater Gin Distillery. Tours begin every other hour from 1 pm to 5 pm on Fridays, and from 11 am to 5 pm on Saturdays and Sundays – advanced booking required, see their website. 1 Leaving the distillery turn left, then left again on to Montford Place. 2 Continue down Kennington Road to Kennington Park. 3 Turn left and head down Kennington Park Road to Kennington tube station on your left. 4 Enter the station and take the Northern line northbound to Leicester Square. Leave using the 1 – National Galleries exit. 5 Crossing the road, turn left and continue on Charing Cross Road, turning left after Wyndham's Theatre. 6 Head straight down this road until you reach St Martin's Lane where you'll see Mr Fogg's Gin Parlour (opposite, bottom) straight ahead. Here, you can enjoy their afternoon 'G & Tea'. Sittings are from 5 pm on Tuesday, Wednesday and Thursday, and from 3 pm on Fridays and 2 pm on Sundays – advanced booking required. Mondays also available from Autumn 2022, enquire via their website.

Mr Fogg's Gin Parlour to The Distillery, Portobello Road

1 Retrace your steps back to Leicester Square tube station and take the Northern line northbound to Tottenham Court Road. 2 Change to the Central line, taking the westbound service to Notting Hill Gate where leave via the third exit (North Side – Portobello Road). 3 Turn right, then right again on to Pembridge Road where you cross and continue straight, taking the first exit on the roundabout on to Kensington Park Road. 4 Cross the road and continue straight until you reach Chepstow Villas where you turn right. 5 Continue on Chepstow Villas, heading straight on at the fork until you reach Portobello Road. 6 Turn left and continue on Portobello Road until you reach Blenheim Crescent. 7 Cross the road and The Distillery will be on the right. Spend the afternoon enjoying G&Ts in GinTonica (open Mon-Fri 12 pm to 10 pm, Sat 11 am to 10 pm and Sun 12 pm to 7 pm), then move to The Resting Room (times may vary, check website), for gin cocktails and an early dinner.

The Distillery, Portobello Road to Martello Hall
1 Retrace your steps back to Notting Hill Gate tube station where you take the Central line eastbound to Liverpool Street. **2** Change here for the Overground service to London Fields. **3** Exit the station and cross the road, turning right on to Mentmore Terrace, then left down Fortescue Avenue. **4** Turn right when you reach Gransden Avenue, then left on to Lamb Lane. **5** Turn right at the fork on to Elizabeth Fry Road and continue straight, crossing Bayford Street before turning left, then right on to Bayford Mews. Martello Hall will be on your left (open Mon-Wed 10 am to 12 am, Thurs 10 am to 2 am, Fri-Sat 10am to 3am, and Sun 12 pm - 11pm).

Summerhall Distillery to 56 North

Begin with a tour of the Summerhall Distillery (**see page 157** for more information – pictured opposite, bottom). Tours are held Thursday to Sunday, and must be booked in advance. **1** Turn right out of the distillery and head up Hope Park Crescent. **2** Cross the main road (Hope Park Terrace) and head straight up Hope Park Crescent. **3** Continue as it becomes Buccleuch Street until you get to W Crosscauseway where you turn right and 56 North will be on your left (open Mon-Sun 11 am to 9 pm).

56 North to One Square

1 Retrace your steps back to Buccleuch Street, turning right on to Chapel Street. Head down Chapel Street, then turn right on to Crichton Street. **2** Take the first right between two Edinburgh University buildings then the first left. Follow the path to the end of the building and turn right then left at the university pharmacy. **3** Continue straight until you reach a T-junction, taking the right fork then follow the path to Lothian Street. **4** Turn left and continue as it becomes Teviot Place, then Lauriston Place. Head straight on until you reach Lauriston Street on the right by the Premier Inn. **5** Cross the road and head down Lauriston Street until you get to West Port where turn left and follow as it becomes Bread Street. **6** Continue until you get to Lothian Road where turn right and head straight on until you get to BrewDog bar. **7** Turn left in front of the bar and follow the path, making a slight right past All Bar One. One Square will be on your left (open Mon-Sun 7 am to 1 am).

One Square to Heads and Tales

1 Retrace your steps back to Lothian Road and turn left. Continue straight until you come to a crossing where take the left turn on to Shandwick Place. **2** Turn left again to stay on Shandwick Place then continue until you reach Edinburgh Gin Distillery/Heads and Tales bar on your left (Edinburgh Gin Distillery is open Mon-Sun 10 am to 4.30 pm, Heads and Tales bar is open Thurs-Sat 5 pm to 3 am).

Heads and Tales to The Jolly Botanist

1 Turn left out of Heads and Tales and head down Shandwick Place until you reach Antholl Crescent where turn left. **2** Follow Antholl Crescent to Coates Crescent where turn left and continue straight as it becomes Antholl Place. **3** When Devil's Scribe Tattoo parlour appears on your left, follow the road round to the left to the main road (Torpichen Street). **4** Cross the road and head straight down Torpichen Place until you reach Morrison Street. **5** Turn right and continue on Morrison Street until you reach The Jolly Botanist on your right (open Mon-Thurs 4 pm to 12 am, Fri 1 pm to 1 am, Sat 12 pm to 1 am and Sun 12 pm to 12 am).

Celtic Whiskey Shop to JT Pim's
Begin at the Celtic Whiskey Shop on Dawson Street (open Mon-Sat
10.30 am to 7 pm, and Sun 12.30 am to 6 pm). **1** After browsing their
extensive selection of gins, leave the shop, turning left up Dawson Street.
2 Head down Dawson Street until you get to Lemon Street. Turn left and
continue straight until you reach Grafton Street. **3** Cross the road and turn
right, then take the first left on to Johnson's Court. **4** Follow the road until
you get to William Street S where you cross and turn right, then immediately
left down Castle Market. **5** Cross the road at Drury Street and continue
straight down George's Street Arcade. **6** Turn right at South Great George's
Street and continue straight, crossing the road to head down Exchequer
Street. JT Pim's will come up on your right (Mon-Thu 12 pm to 11.30 pm,
Fri-Sat 12 pm to 1 am and Sun 12 pm to 11 pm).

JT Pim's to The Bull and Castle
1 Turn right as you come out of JT Pim's and continue up South Great
George's Street until you get to Dame Street where you turn left. Head down
Dame Street as it turns into Lord Edward Street. **2** Continue to T-junction
opposite Christ Church Cathedral. **3** Turn left on to Christchurch Place and
The Bull and Castle will come up on the left (open Mon-Thurs 12 pm to 10
pm, Fri-Sat 12 pm to 11 pm and Sun 12.30 pm to 9 pm).

The Bull and Castle to Street 66
1 Retrace your steps up Christchurch Place and head back down Lord
Edward Street until you reach Parliament Street. **2** Turn left and continue
straight until Street 66 (opposite) comes up on the left (Mon-Thu
3 pm to 11.30 am, Fri 3 pm to 2.30 am and Sat 3 pm to 1.30 am, Sun 3 pm
to 11.30 pm).

Street 66 to The Gin Palace

1 Turn left out of Street 66 and continue up Parliament Street until you reach the waterfront, opposite Grattan Bridge. **2** Crossing the main road turn right, following the road to Millennium Bridge. **3** Cross the bridge then cross the road. **4** Turn right, heading down Ormond Quay Lower until you reach Liffey Street Lower where turn left. 5. Follow the road to Middle Abbey Street where turn right and The Gin Palace Dublin will come up on your right (Mon-Wed 3 pm to 11.30 pm, Thurs-Sun 12.30 pm - 12.30 am).

USING THE GUIDE

Name of bar/distillery.

Region in which the bar/ distillery is located.

City, town or village and county, in which the bar/ distillery is located.

Type of establishment.

The botanicals used to make each distillery's main craft gin are listed, starting with juniper.

Postal address and other key information.

Review.

Opening hours as we went to press – check online.

Places of interest near the bar/distillery.

THE SOUTH-WEST

Scilly Spirit Distillery

St Mary's Island, Isles of Scilly
Distillery, shop and gin school

ESSENTIAL INFORMATION
Key botanicals (Island Gin): juniper, cardamom, cassia bark, kaffir lime leaf, orange peel, fennel seed, pink peppercorns
Output: 12,000 bottles a year
Location: Old Town Lane, St Mary's, Isles of Scilly, TR21 0NN
Telephone: 01720 422400
Email: hello@scillyspirit.com
Website: www.scillyspirit.com
Facebook: www.facebook.com/scillyspirit
Instagram: @scillyspirit
Twitter: @scillyspirit

Opening hours:
Monday-Friday 0930-1630
Saturday 0930-1230
Distillery Tours: Tuesday 1530 and 1630
    Friday 1030 and 1130
Gin School: Tuesday 1130-1430
    Friday 1400-1700

Other reasons to go:
Isles of Scilly archipelago, boat trip to Bishop Rock Lighthouse, beaches, rare wildlife species, local artists, galleries, restaurants, hotels

At the most south-westerly point of the UK, husband and wife team Arthur and Hilary Miller established their Scilly Spirit Distillery on St Mary's Island in the enchanting Isles of Scilly. The distillery opened May 2019, and they were quickly receiving many impressive awards within weeks of releasing their Island Gin.

When they were developing their brand, the inspiration for their Island Gin (below) stemmed from an event way back on 18th January 1665, when a spice trade ship was wrecked off their local Bishop Rock, carrying peppercorns from Java. Peppercorn therefore feature as a key botanical.

The outstanding beauty of the Isles of Scilly and its seaside heritage provided founders Arthur and Hilary with a rich territory to inspire their bottle design. They pay homage to the lighthouse which stands on Bishop Rock through the bottle's shape and the aqua-green colour captures the Scilly seas and uses imagery of the local Western Rocks. Even their tamper seal was designed as a reference to the pilot gig boats, a key part of Scilly's heritage.

They launched a Navy Strength Gin in November 2020, naming it Atlantic Strength (opposite, top left, left bottle), because Arthur and Hilary hand pick the wild Atlantic fennel which grows along the island's coastline. In October 2021, they released their Rosé aged gin (opposite, top right) which is barrel-aged in former port casks to deliver the tawny red colour, with a hint of dry vermouth on the palate. They worked with artist Oriel Hicks from a local gallery to replicate her glass work of the sunset over Samson for the label on the back of the clear Rosé Island Gin 50cl bottles. View it through the bottle and you experience a rosy good-weather gin sunset

Design excellence aside, the gin itself was awarded Gold at the 2022 International Wine and Spirit Challenge – one of only 16 UK distillers to receive such an award from the 1,200 gins entered.

The duo still complete every aspect of making their three Island Gins: from the small-batch distillation runs to bottling and labelling, packing and dispatch of website orders. Not to mention fulfilling all trade shipments, loading their gins on to the thrice-weekly freight ship to Penzance.

These local, authentic, artisan gins showcase their owners' total commitment. Try their Island Gins in person, an excuse to enjoy the beautiful Isles of Scilly while you sip.

LOCATION MAPS

SOUTH-WEST ENGLAND, WALES, WEST MIDLANDS

Aberdaron

Dyfi 86

Cardigan Bay

Aberystwyth

Aberaeron

Tregaron

Cardigan

Newport

Lampeter

Llandysul 88

St. David's

Carmarthen

Haverfordwest

Narberth

Pontarddulais

Pembroke

Llanelli

Carmarthen Bay

SWANSEA 89

Bristol

Barnstaple

Hartland Pt.

Hartland

Great Torrington

Bude

Wadebridge

Callington

Liskeard 42

PLYMOUTH 44

St. Ives

Redruth

Truro

Ponsanooth 46

Salcombe 48

Land's End

Mount's Bay

St Mary's Island 50

Lizard Pt.

18

Ruthin · Chester
Crewe
Wrexham 91
Llanfyllin
Market Drayton 102
Telford
Cannock
Llangurig
Knighton
Ludlow 100
COVENTRY
Penybont
Leominster
Ladayder
M42
M5
M40
Brecon
Stratford-upon-Avon 112
West Midlands 114
Ebbw Vale
Cheltenham 97
Pontypool
Cirencester 95
Pontypridd
Caerphilly 85
NEWPORT
SWINDON
BRISTOL 33
BATH 31
Channel
Burnham-on-Sea
Street
Exmoor 40
Sherborne
Illompton
Exeter 39
Fordington 41
Christchurch 35
Exmouth
Weymouth
Swanage
Dartmouth 37
Bill of Portland

Sutton-on-the-Forest 150
Norton
Great Driffield
YORK
Pocklington
A166
Skipton
Kettlewell
Settle
BLACKBURN
Burnley 127
Longridge 148
Preston 132
Penwortham 130
KINGSTON-UPON-HULL
Leyland
M62
Dewsbury
Thorne
M18
Scunthorpe
M6
Holmfirth 129
M62
BARNSLEY
M180
WIGAN
MANCHESTER
DONCASTER
A628
LIVERPOOL
M57
SHEFFIELD 134-136
Gainsborough
A631
Wilmslow
Retford
Spital 137
Chester
Macclesfield
Chesterfield
A623
Kelsall 147
Leek
Sutton-in-Ashfield
Newark-on-Trent
A617
Crewe
M6
Newcastle-under-Lyme
A51
Sleaford
A52
Stoke
Ambergate 92
NOTTINGHAM 108
Folkingham
DERBY
Ruddington 110
A52
M6
Stafford
Loughborough
Melton Mowbray
Bourne
A511
Nanpantan 106
A46
Cannock
Tamworth
LEICESTER
A47
A6003
M6
BIRMINGHAM
Market Harborough 104
Corby
Kettering
COVENTRY
M42
M40
Rugby
Wellingborough
Northampton
A428
Redditch
Bedford
Sandy 75
Stratford-upon-Avon 112
Edgehill 98
MILTON KEYNES
A421
LUTON
M40
A41
Wilstone 80
Buckinghamshire 94
High Wycombe
Watford
M40
SWINDON
M4
SLOUGH
M5
BRISTOL 33
READING
BRACKNELL
BATH 31
Newbury
A4
Devizes
A338
Basingstoke
Aldershot
Albury 52
M3
Farnham
Longparish 82
Street
Amesbury
Haslemere
Winchester 84
A272
SOUTHAMPTON 101
M27
Chichester 58-60
PORTSMOUTH 74
Bognor Regis
BOURNEMOUTH 32

20

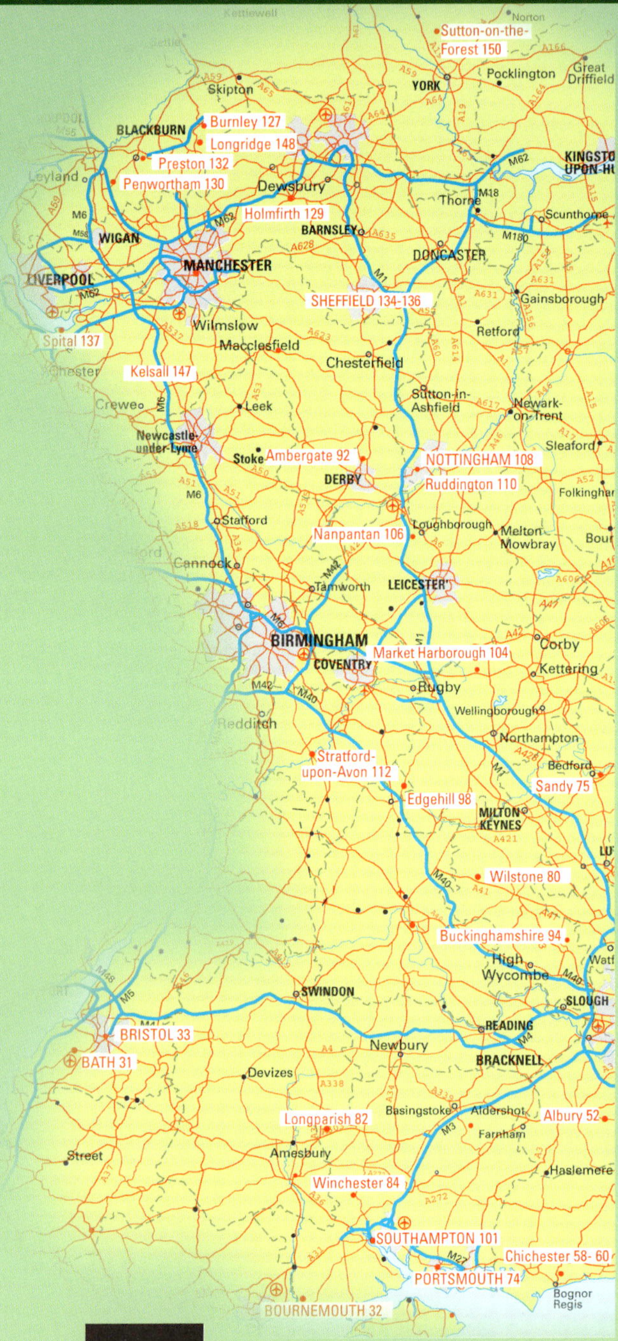

SOUTH-EAST
ENGLAND,
THE MIDLANDS,
EAST ANGLIA,
NORTHERN
ENGLAND

Withernsea

Grimsby

Mablethorpe

Horncastle
A158   A158

Coningsby   Skegness

Boston   Hunstanton

Donington

Wisbech   Cromer

Fakenham 117   Wroxham

March   NORWICH 122-125   Great Yarmouth

Chatteris   Mundford   Lowestoft

Brandon

Huntingdon 119   Thetford

Burwell

CAMBRIDGE 115   Newmarket 121

Royston   Claydon

Sudbury 126

Stevenage   Braintree

Stansted   Clacton-on-Sea

Palmer's Green 72

Highgate 64   Rayleigh

Haggerston 63

LONDON 66-69

Brixton 57   Bermondsey 53-55   Herne Bay

Banstead   Thames Estuary

Reigate   Canterbury

Dorking 61   Tonbridge 78

Marden 70

Brighton 56   Seaford 76   Eastbourne

LOCATION MAPS

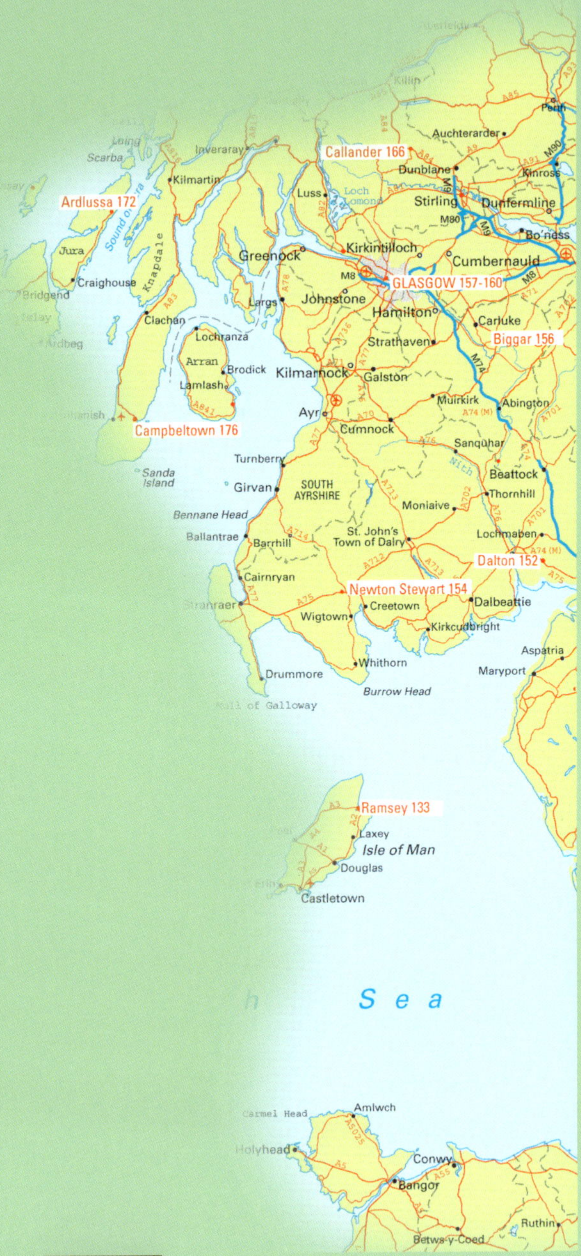

NORTHERN ENGLAND, SCOTLAND

Forfar
Lunan Bay
Glamis 168
Inverkeilor 170
Arbroath
Carnoustie
DUNDEE
St. Andrews Bay
A92
A91
A915
Fife Ness
Leven
Isle of May
Kirkcaldy
Firth of Forth
North Berwick 165
EDINBURGH 161-164
Grantshouse
Penicuik
Ayton
Lauder
A682
Greenlaw
A698
Galashiels
Kelso 153
Wooler
A708
Hawick
Alnwick 139
A68
Amble
Kielder Water
Otterburn
A697
Langholm
A68
Longtown
Whitley Bay
Haltwhistle
GATESHEAD **SUNDERLAND**
Gretna
A686
Consett
A69
Alston
Durham 145
Stanhope
A689
Tees
Whitby
Brough
A66
Stokesley
A59
Colburn 141
Northallerton
A684
Bedale 143
Kettlewell
Bridlington
A64
A166
Lancaster
A65
Fleetwood
BLACKPOOL M55
A163
KINGSTON UPON HULL
Ormskirk
Huddersfield
M18
Scunthorpe
M6
WIGAN
A635
Brigg
LIVERPOOL
MANCHESTER
A628
SHEFFIELD
M1
Gainsborough
A631
Knutsford
Wilmslow
Worksop
A616
M56
Chester

23

SCOTLAND

Portnaguran
Stornoway

Kebock Head

Taransay
Toe Head
Harris
Berneray
Rodel
Vallay
North Uist
Lochmaddy
Benbecula
Ronay
Wiay
South Uist
Lochboisdale
Eriskay
Barra
Castlebay
Vatersay
Sandray
Rosinish
Mingulay
Berneray

The Minch
The Little Minch
Outer Hebrides
Sea of the Hebrides

Cape Wrath
Durness
Handa I.
Scourie
Pt. of Stoer
Eriboll
L. Hope
Tongue
Loch Loyal
Loch Stack
Altnaharra
Loch Naver
Enard
Inchnadamph
Lochinver
Loch Shin
Lairg
Rubha Cóigeach
Greenstone Pt.
Bonar Bridge

Poolewe
Fionn Loch
Badachro 174
Lochan Fada
Alness
Staffin
Rona
Achnasheen
Garve
Dunvegan
Sound of Raasay
Torridon
Shieldaig
Skye
Raasay
Lochcarron
Loch Monar
Beauly
Sligachan
Stromeferry
Cannich
Broadford
Kyleakin
Invermoriston
Ardvasar
Loch Cluanie
Fort Augustus
Canna
Invergarry
Rùm
Mallaig
Loch Quoich
Loch Lochy
Dalwhinnie
Eigg
Glenfinnan
Loch Arkaig
Muck
Loch Shiel
Acharacle
Loch Ericht
Coll
North Ballachulish 183
Loch Rannoch
Tobermory
Hynish 182
Lochaline
Bridge of Orchy
Craignure
Oban
Tyndrum
Lochearnhead
Iona
Fionnphort
Mull
Dalmally
Kilninver
Inveraray
Cairndow

Inner Sound

A855 A836 A838 A894 A897 A838 A836 A835 A832 A890 A87 A830 A82 A828 A85 A819 A889

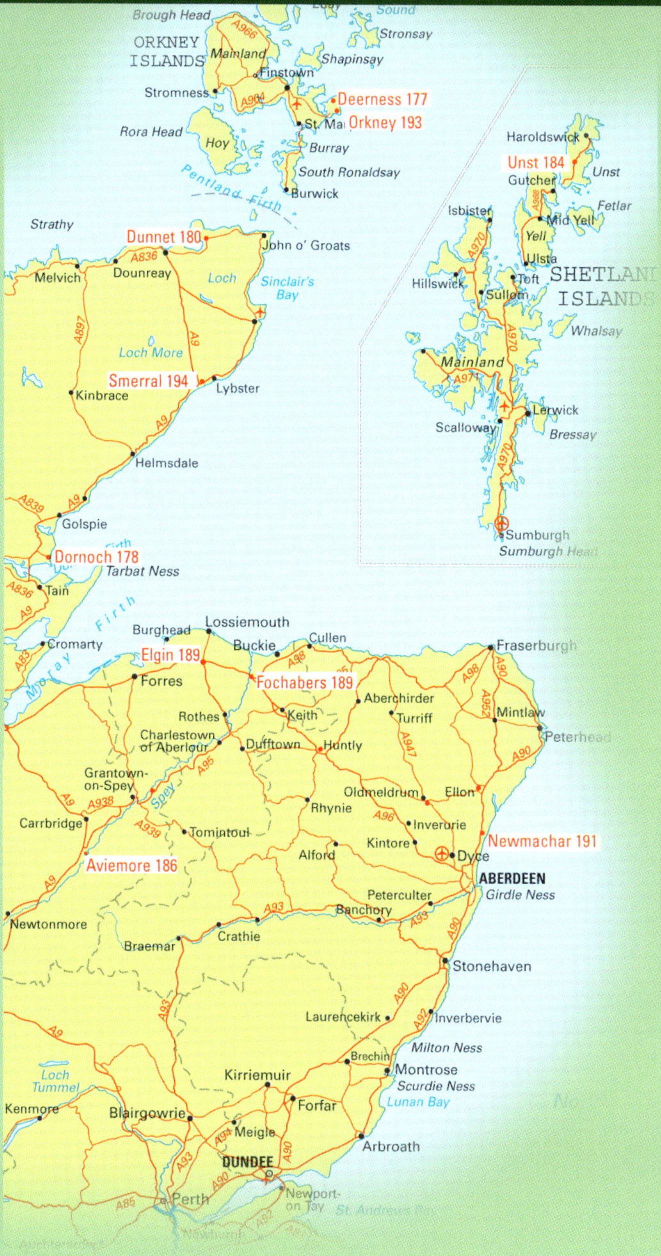

Brough Head
Egg Sound
Stronsay
ORKNEY ISLANDS
Mainland
Shapinsay
Finstown
Stromness
A904
Deerness 177
Orkney 193
St. Ma
Rora Head
Hoy
Burray
South Ronaldsay
Burwick
Haroldswick
Unst 184
Unst
Gutcher
Fetlar
Strathy
Isbister
Mid Yell
Dunnet 180
A836
Yell
Melvich
Dounreay
Loch
Sinclair's Bay
Ulsta
SHETLAND ISLANDS
John o' Groats
Hillswick
Toft
A887
A9
Sullom
Whalsay
Loch More
Smerral 194
Kinbrace
Lybster
A970
A9
Mainland
A971
Helmsdale
Lerwick
A839
A9
Scalloway
Bressay
Golspie
Firth
Dornoch 178
Tarbat Ness
A9
A836
Tain
Sumburgh
Sumburgh Head
A970
Firth
Burghead
Lossiemouth
Cromarty
A9
Forres
Elgin 189
Buckie
Cullen
Fraserburgh
Moray
Fochabers 189
Aberchirder
A98
Rothes
Keith
Turriff
Mintlaw
Charlestown of Aberlour
Dufftown
Huntly
A952
Peterhead
Grantown-on-Spey
Spey
A947
A96
Oldmeldrum
Ellon
A90
Carrbridge
A9
A938
A939
Tomintoul
Rhynie
Inverurie
A96
Newmachar 191
Aviemore 186
A95
Alford
Kintore
Dyce
Newtonmore
Alford
ABERDEEN
Peterculter
Girdle Ness
Braemar
A93
Crathie
Banchory
A93
A90
Stonehaven
A9
Laurencekirk
A90
Inverbervie
Milton Ness
Loch Tummel
Brechin
Montrose
Kenmore
Kirriemuir
Scurdie Ness
Lunan Bay
Blairgowrie
Forfar
A93
A94
Meigle
A90
DUNDEE
Arbroath
A90
A89
Perth
Newport-on-Tay
St. Andrews Bay

LOCATION MAPS

NORTHERN IRELAND
REPUBLIC OF IRELAND

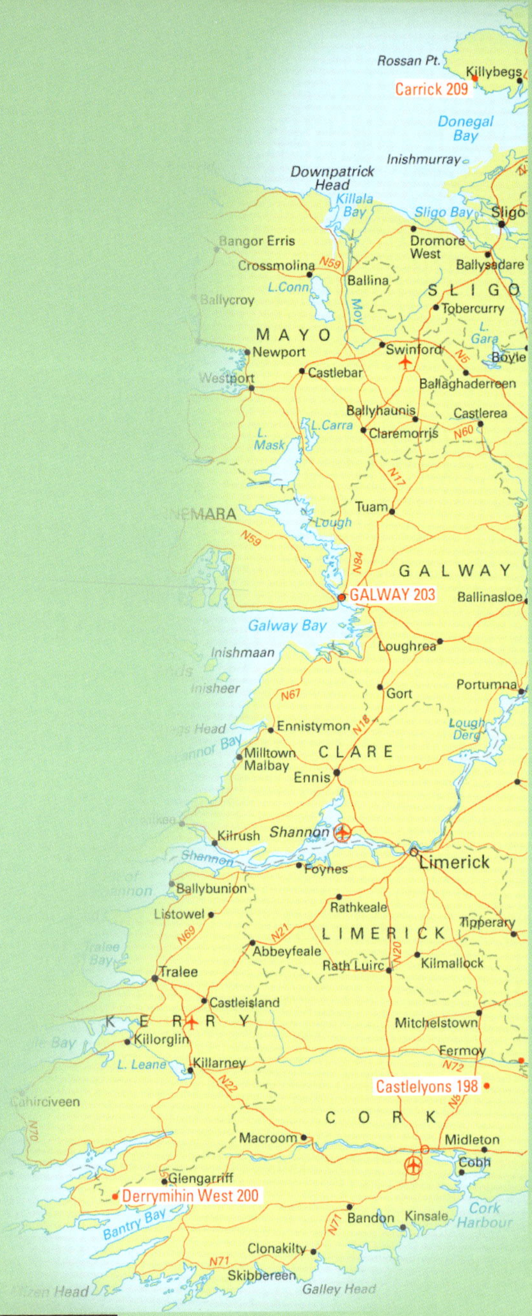

Rossan Pt.
Killybegs
Carrick 209

Donegal Bay

Inishmurray

Downpatrick Head

Killala Bay

Sligo Bay — Sligo

Dromore West
Ballysadare

Bangor Erris
Crossmolina
Ballina
L.Conn
Ballycroy

S L I G O
Tobercurry

L. Gara

MAYO
Newport
Castlebar
Swinford
Boyle
Westport
Ballaghaderreen

Ballyhaunis
Castlerea
L.Carra
Claremorris
L. Mask

Tuam
Lough

NEMARA

GALWAY
GALWAY 203
Ballinasloe

Galway Bay
Loughrea

Inishmaan
Inisheer
Gort
Portumna

s Head
Ennistymon
Lough Derg

Milltown Malbay
C L A R E
Ennis

Kilrush
Shannon
Shannon
Foynes
Limerick
Ballybunion

Listowel
Rathkeale
Tipperary

Abbeyfeale
L I M E R I C K
Tralee Bay
Rath Luirc
Kilmallock

Tralee
Castleisland
Mitchelstown
Fermoy

K E R R Y
Killorglin
Killarney
Castlelyons 198

Cahirciveen
C O R K
Macroom
Midleton
Cobh

Glengarriff
Derrymihin West 200
Bandon
Kinsale
Cork Harbour

Bantry Bay
Clonakilty
Skibbereen
Galley Head

26

DONEGAL
Glenties
Ballybofey
Strabane
Ballymena
Magherafelt
Donegal
Omagh
NORTHERN
Cookstown
Antrim
Lough
Carrickfergus
Bangor
Ballyshannon
IRELAND
Neagh
Donaghadee
Bundoran
Dungannon
Newtownards
Lower
Irvinestown
A32
Dungannon
ARDS
L. Erne
FERMANAGH
Manorhamilton
Enniskillen 196
Blackwater
Dromore
Crossgar 195
Strangford
Upper
Armagh
Downpatrick
Ardglass
Monaghan
A28
Clones
Newry
Newcastle
Drumshanbo 202
MONAGHAN
L. Key
Belturbet
Warrenpoint
Kilkeel
LEITRIM
Cavan
Carrickmacross
Carrick-on-
CAVAN
Dundalk
Ballagan Pt.
Shannon
Dundalk Bay
Virginia
LOUTH
Longford
Sheelin
Ceanannus
Clogher Head
Roscommon
Mor (Kells)
Drogheda
Bay
Lanesborough 206
Drogheda 204
Lough
Royal
Navan
Balbriggan
Ree
Mullingar
Trim
Boyne
Athlone
WEST MEATH
Moate
MEATH
DUBLIN
Kinnegad
Swords
N6
M4 Lucan
M1
N4
M50
Grand Canal
Tullamore 207
Dun Laoghaire
OFFALY
KILDARE
Droichead
M7
Portarlington
Nua
Naas
M11
Bray
Birr
Mountmellick
Monasterevin
M9
Poulaphouca
Res.
N7
Portlaoise
Roscrea
Mountrath
Athy
Barrow
Wicklow
LAOIS
Abbyleix
WICKLOW
Rathdrum
Templemore
Carlow
Mizen Head
Thurles
Tullow
Arklow
CARLOW
TIPPERARY
Kilkenny
Slaney
Callan
KILKENNY
Cahore
Thomastown
Point
Enniscorthy
Cahir
Carrick-
WEXFORD
on-Suir
New
Clonmel
Ross
Wexford
Waterford
Rosslare
WATERF
Tramore
Dungarvan
Helvick Head
Waterford
Hook
Harbour
Head
Youghal
Youghal
Bay

GLOSSARY

bathtub method the botanicals are prepard by hand and slowly steeped in a neutral, bought-in grain spirit

genever the juniper-flavoured national spirit of Holland from which gin evolved. Also known as Dutch Gin, it's traditionally made with a grape-based spirit

head the first vapours to boil off the alcohol during distillation, containing volatile alcohols such as methanol

heart the 'middle' vapours to boil off during distillation, containing primarily ethanol, the most desirable compound of alcohol

tail the final vapours to boil off the alcohol during distillation, which have a bitter flavour

multi-shot method the botanicals are distilled individually so they stand out in their own right rather than thrown into a single distillation together

one-shot method all the botanicals are macerated in the neutral base spirit before they are heated

perfect serve the best combination of mixer, garnish and glassware to complement the spirit

rotary evaporation method botanicals are distilled with the base spirit in a vaccumed flask which rotates in a warm bath

vacuum (or cold) distillation method distilling in a vacuum. This creates a lower boiling point for the alcohol, so the botanicals aren't stewed

vapour infusion method botanicals are placed in a basket above the base spirit which infuses with the botanicals as it evaporates

REPORTING TO THE GUIDE

Please write and tell us about your experience of gin distilleries and bars whether good or bad, whether listed in this edition or not.

The address to write to us is:
Print editor, Duncan Petersen Publishing Ltd
G9, 80 Silverthorne Road,
London,
SW8 3HE

Checklist
Please use a separate sheet of paper for each report; include your name, address and telephone number on each report.

Your reports will be received with particular pleasure if they are typed, and if they are organized under the following headings:

Name of establishment
Town or village it is in, or nearest
Full address, including postcode
The building and setting
Atmosphere, welcome and service

We assume that in writing you have no objection to your views being published unpaid, either verbatim or in an edited version. Names of major outside contributors are acknowledged, at the editor's discretion, in the guide.

Gin Spotlight: Anno Extreme 95 'The World's Strongest Gin'

Created by Anno in 2020, Anno Extreme 95 packs a punch at a staggering 95% ABV, and can claim to be the world's strongest gin.

While the alcoholic content is what draws the crowds, the team at Anno have put that scientific expertise to good use once again. With a high alcoholic content it could be easy to lose nuance of flavour, but once mixed with a good tonic the Extreme 95 is surprisingly smooth and easy-drinking, with grapefruit, eucalyptus, and nutmeg botanicals giving way to a warming heat from spices and big juniper flavours.

One of the great things about the spirit – other than being able to say you've tried the world's strongest gin, of course – is that you only need a small amount in order to achieve big flavour. Just 5 ml will achieve the same flavour balance as your average G&T, and each bottle comes with a little 25 ml measure to help you get your quantities just right.

See page 70 for Anno Distiller's full entry.

The Bath Botanical Gin Distillery and Herbal Apothecary

Bath, Somerset

Distillery

ESSENTIAL INFORMATION
Key botanicals (No.1 Gin): juniper, coriander, liquorice, star anise, lemon peel, Somerset lime flower
Output: 50 litres every two weeks
Location: 1A Prior Park Road, Widcombe, Bath, BA2 4NG
Telephone: 01225 635782
Email: mullettsue@gmail.com
Website: www.bathbotanics.co.uk
Facebook: www.facebook.com/BathBotanicalGinDistillery
Instagram: @bathbotanicalgindistillery

Opening hours:
Thursday-Saturday 1300-1730

Other reasons to go: The Roman Baths, Bath Abbey, Pulteney Bridge

An intelligent twist on the gin microdistillery concept: Sue Mullett, who has an MSc in herbal medicine, distils not just regular gin but gin that will cure all ailments: alcohol extracts the essence of herbal remedies much better than water. Her ordinary gins are in clear bottles, and the herbal range in clay bottles. Taste the regular flavouring and medicinal extracts through a straw, or taste the finished gins from a small glass. The Somerset lime flowers used in No.1 are hand-foraged locally.

Alongside the regular gins she sells seasonal fruit gins grown on local biodynamic farms – which have an organic, holistic approach 'reliant on the ecological health of the farmland to grow crops in tandem with the astrological cycle.'

Then there are Sue's speciality gins such as Christmas Gin flavoured with cocoa, orange and cinnamon; or No.2 Grapefruit, infused with fresh pink grapefruit to make a bitter-sweet citrus gin.

This is a tasting and retail outlet only. As well as the gins, they sell kits for making your own botanical gin at home.

Conker Gin and Conker Spirit

Bournemouth, Dorset
Distillery

ESSENTIAL INFORMATION

Key botanicals (Conker Dorset Dry Gin):
   juniper, lime, elderberries, samphire, gorse

Output: not disclosed

Location: Unit 2, 163 Stourvale Road,
   Bournemouth, BH6 5HQ

Telephone: 01202 430384

Email: hello@conkerspirit.co.uk

Website: www.conkerspirit.co.uk

Facebook: www.facebook.com/
   Conkerdistillery

Instagram: @conkerdistillery

Opening hours:

Monday-Thursday 0900-1700

Friday 0800-1600

Other reasons to go: Bournemouth Parks,
Boscombe Chine Gardens

David Smith writes: Conker Spirit was founded in 2014 by Rupert Holloway as Dorset's first distillery, but since then it's been joined by half a dozen others.

Conker Dorset Dry Gin was released in 2015 and is made using ten botanicals, including three that are locally sourced in Dorset: elderberries, samphire, and gorse flowers. There's also English coriander from Sussex in the gin, which is proofed down to bottling strength using spring water from the nearby New Forest.

The distillery's second release was a Cold Brew Coffee Liqueur, which was followed in 2018 by two limited edition gins: a port-cask aged gin and a navy strength gin. Conker Navy Strength Gin is a tweaked version of their original gin, without the gorse flowers, and £5 from each sale is donated to the RNLI.

In 2017, Conker Spirit partnered with local rum expert Peter Holland and That Boutique-y Gin Company to create Mojito Gin which has a molasses base, similar to rum, and botanical flavours including lime and fresh mint.

Conker Distillery is located about 15 minutes walk from Pokesdown railway station and is open to visitors for Tours and Tap Room (book online) fortnightly on a Friday. The tours are conducted by Conker's head distiller who gives a talk on the entire gin production process, from botanicals to bottle, and guides you through a tasting of Conker's products.

Psychopomp Microdistillery

Bristol
Distillery and tasting room

ESSENTIAL INFORMATION

Key botanicals (Wōden Gin): juniper, coriander seed, cassia bark, grapefruit zest, fennel seed

Output: 15,000 bottles a year

Location: 145 St Michael's Hill, Bristol, BS2 8DB

Telephone: 07511 934675

Email: info@microdistillery.co.uk

Website: www.microdistillery.co.uk

Facebook: www.facebook.com/microdistillery

Instagram: @microdistillery

Twitter: @PsychopompMD

Opening hours:
Monday-Saturday 1200-1700

Other reasons to go: Bristol Museum and Art Gallery, Cabot Tower, Bristol Cathedral

St Michael's Hill is a cool corner of Bristol, a student area with a university building at its foot. Shops are mostly independent and quirky. Psychopomp Microdistillery is probably the most individual and interesting of them all. You need to look twice to spot it because the original shop sign (next page, top left) still dominates – 'A. Jenkins Groceries – Provisions'.

Psychopomp is a small, independent, carbon-neutral microdistillery. They use handmade 30L copper pot stills to make gin in small batches using a single shot method (see page 28). They make their signature gin recipe 'Wōden' alongside limited edition seasonal recipes, an 'Old Tom', and bespoke batches for independent restaurants and producers.

In true craft fashion, Psychopomp was never 'founded' – it just sort of happened. Owners Liam and Danny started as hobby distillers, building gin stills in their basement and experimenting with recipes for years before officially forming a company in 2014. From their basement to their current home in 'A. Jenkins', they have always worked in small spaces and have never stopped experimenting. Alongside their signature gins, they produce a variety of other unique spirits; the first British aquavit, a Parisian style absinthe and a single origin coffee digestif.

In ancient mythology, a Psychopomp was the spiritual guide of a living person's soul.

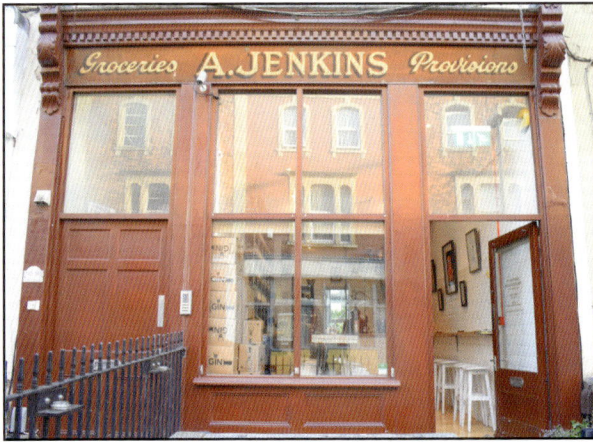

The team name their core range after different psychopomps from around the world. For example, 'Wōden' is the Anglo-Saxon counterpart of the Norse god Odin (after whom Wednesday is named). The distillery hosts a variety of experiences, including weekly gin tasting masterclasses and distilling workshops.

Pothecary Blue Label Gin and Soapbox Spirits Ltd

Christchurch, Dorset
Distillery

ESSENTIAL INFORMATION

Key botanicals (Pothecary Blue Label Gin):
juniper, lemon peel, black mulberry, lavender, lime flowers

Output: <5,000 bottles a year

Location: 91 Stour Road, Christchurch, BH23 1JN

Telephone: 07534 804917

Email: martin.soapboxspirits@gmail.com

Website: www.pothecarygin.co.uk

Facebook: www.facebook.com/PothecaryGin

Instagram: @pothecarygin

Twitter: @PothecaryGin

Opening hours:
By appointment only

Other reasons to go: Avon Beach, Mudeford Quay, Chistchurch Castle, Highcliffe Beach

Methodical, thorough, inspired: a fair summary of Martin Jennings's (next page, bottom) and business partner Lucas's approach. Both have a background in the wine, spirit and hospitality industries and both did seven months' homework at trade events while waiting for HMRC to process their licence – plenty of time to work out what their niche would be.

Launched in 2016, their gins have won a multitude of awards including SFSC Double-Gold, CWSA Gold, Best Contemporary Gin UK 2017 in the World Gin Awards, Europe Trophy Double-Gold, plus local/regional awards.

They found that most of the gins they liked best were made in a multi-shot rather than the London Dry process. In multi-shot, the botanicals are distilled so they stand out individually rather than thrown into a single distillation together. The London Dry process distils botanicals together and relies on angelica and orris root to stop the flavours bleeding into each other, which in Martin's view means less clarity of the overall aroma and flavour.

Starting with around 90 botanicals, they set about a rigorous elimination process. With flavour, aroma and texture as the priority, first they sacked about 50 because they were "one-dimensional" – these included coriander, angelica and orris root. Then the remaining 40 were reduced to 25.

After that it became a question of personal preference, and which flavours complemented each other best.

Martin's 27-year wine background made him keenest on the aromatics but he was also looking for an enjoyable taste on the palate and a clean aftertaste to keep the drinker wanting more.

Martin wanted a flavour that breaks through even if heavily diluted, but would also be good as a sipping gin or as a Dry Martini. The last botanical knocked out was fennel because it overpowered the others. The final five are listed opposite under 'key botanicals' and are the ingredients that make Pothecary Blue Label (top right and previous page, middle bottle) an award winner.

Soapbox also produce some limited edition gins. In June 2017, they released 982 bottles of Pothecary Gin Sicilian Blend (previous page, far right bottle), made with oranges, lemons, almonds and gentian root. In February 2018 they launched Pothecary Gin Thai Blend (previous page, far left bottle), using mango, pineapple, lime, coconut, coriander, turmeric root and ginger root to create a subtly spicy, yet fresh and fruity gin. Their latest launch in 2021 was Cromwell's Ruin Gin (top left), created with foraged elderflower and wild chamomile for a sweet floral effect, evoking summer meadows. They also produce bespoke gins for clients.

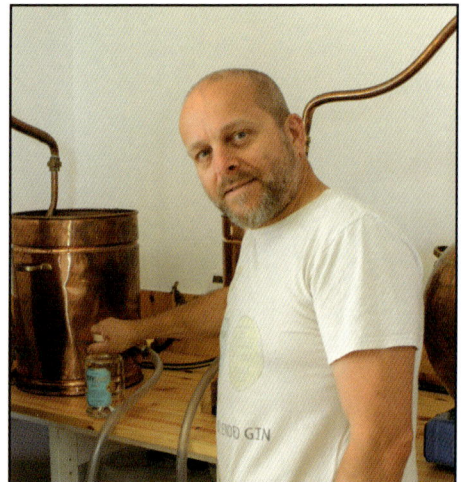

The gins sell through local and national wholesalers, independent retailers and farm shops. This interesting distillery does not sell over the counter, and visits are by appointment only.

Dartmouth English Gin and Dartmouth Distillery

Dartmouth, South Devon

Distillery and gin school

ESSENTIAL INFORMATION

Key botanicals (English Gin): juniper, coriander, liquorice root, cardamom, grains of paradise, cubeb berries, orange peel, lemon peel, grapefruit peel, rosemary, lavender, rose petals, kaffir lime leaves, scots pine needles
Output: 12,000-15,000 bottles a year
Location: Calancombe Estate, South Devon
Telephone: 01548 830905
Email: lance@dartmouth-gin.com
Website: www.dartmouth-gin.com
Facebook: www.facebook.com/ dartmouthgin
Instagram: @Dartmouth.gin
Twitter: @English_gin

Opening hours:
Thursday-Sunday 1100-1700

Other reasons to go: the Calancombe Vineyard holds wine tasting, tours, high-class dining, cream teas and warm welcome

Winner of the 2018 Craft Gin of the Year, Dartmouth English Gin (below right) became a firm favourite of connoisseurs around the world, with a reputation for smoothness and full flavour. The distillery's gins can be enjoyed on their own, are delightful with tonic and are the perfect foundation for a wide range of cocktails.

The unique Müller Brennereianlagen still, purpose-built in Germany's Black Forest for Dartmouth Distillery, creates a beautifully smooth spirit. Using top-quality botanicals gathered from around the world, as well as those grown on the local Calancombe Estate, these gins are made in a slow, patient process that produces classic juniper-led spirits.

Dartmouth Distillery has strong environmental credentials, providing financial support to the Marine Conservation Society and the Seahorse Trust, and it is a founding shareholder in Climeworks, who build and operate carbon capture machines. The distillery is powered by solar panels and their low-carbon production was rewarded by Lux Life Magazine's award of 2021's Leading Carbon-Neutral Gin Producer in the UK.

In this now crowded market, Dartmouth English Gins have been singled out by leading commentators such as Spirits Kiosk who say: 'With lavender, rose, rosemary and lime leaves in the mix, it is one of the best we've tried in years. The gentle lavender and rose, fragrant herbs and a splash of citrus juice cutting through the crisp pine make Dartmouth Gin one of the best G&T gins on the market. Serve with Indian tonic and a rosemary and grapefruit garnish.'

Olivier Ward, Editor of the Gin Foundry, describes it as 'a truly special contemporary classic ranked in the top tier of Dry Gins anywhere in the world. There's bright citrus, soft florals, clear gin heart and a lingering finish. The perfectly layered journey is a treat to the senses. A must have.' The photos: above, Dartmouth estuary; right, the gold labels; below, the gin school.

Crocketts

Exeter, Devon
Bar

Ella Carr writes: This elegant gin bar (bottom left) can be found in the historic Gandy Street area of Exeter's bustling cultural quarter – rumoured to have been the inspiration for Diagon Alley in the *Harry Potter* books. Indeed, Crocketts' Grade II-listed building shares something of the faded grandeur of Grimmauld Place, with lovely antique chandeliers hanging from its 'Library' upstairs, and quirky curios adorning its two floors.

Having housed a clothes shop for many years, the building has gone back to its roots. It's located on the same spot where William Crockett, a wine and spirit merchant in the 1840s, sold his wares (he also happened to be Mayor of Exeter in 1823).

A bespoke handmade copper bar takes centre stage along the length of the cosy ground floor drinking area, behind which glisten a collection of 200 gins (and counting). Their speciality is artisan gins distilled across the South-West, with a collection which holds both familiar and obscure names. Expect to see stalwarts such as Hendricks, Aviation Gin and Brooklyn Gin sitting alongside the weird and wonderful, such as gins that change colour, and even one distilled with collagen (and other anti-ageing botanicals). Taking pride of place at the centre of the back bar is their own mini gin still, named Billy.

The knowledgeable bartenders will guide you through the gins, and the bar regularly hosts gin talks and tastings from local distillers. If by chance you enter unsure of what you think about gin, we guarantee that you'll leave a convert.

Wicked Wolf Gin

Exmoor, Devon
Distillery

ESSENTIAL INFORMATION

Key botanicals (Wicked Wolf Exmoor Gin): juniper, coriander, cardamom, cubeb, grains of paradise, lemon peel, orange peel, kaffir lime leaf, hibiscus, lemongrass

Output: up to 23,400 bottles a year

Location: The Old Chapel Brendon Ltd, T/A Wicked Wolf, Brendon, Exmoor, EX35 6PT

Telephone: 01598 741357

Email: info@wickedwolfgin.com

Website: www.wickedwolfgin.com

Facebook: www.facebook.com/wickedwolfgin

Instagram: @wickedwolfgin

Opening hours: not open to the public

Wicked Wolf's tagline, 'The spirit of Exmoor', is apt: it's distilled and blended on the banks of the East Lyn river, which rises on Exmoor. Co-founders and husband and wife Pat Patel and Julie Heap met at university in Falmouth and afterwards worked in London at design and branding agencies. Almost 20 years later, they moved back to the South-west, aiming to set up a business that would allow them to work from home. They wanted to do something in the food and drink industry, and initially looked at opening a smokehouse but rejected the idea because of cost and fears there were already too many.

However, with the gin renaissance in full swing, and being fans of the spirit themselves, they decided to have a crack at craft gin. They knew their product had to be different, so opted for Asian flavours, including cardamom, kaffir lime leaves, lemongrass and hibiscus. Hibiscus gives the gin its sweet taste and is a replacement for liquorice, which is considered the marmite of botanicals – you either love it or hate it.

They run their copper, gas-powered stills deliberately slow for maximum flavour and strength. Since launching in 2016, they've added more gins and a vodka to their range. All their gins feature their own key botanicals. Full Moon (42%) has mango and cracked black pepper; 1869 (42%) has meadowsweet, whortleberries (bilberries), heather and vanilla; Exmoor Gold Gin uses Exmoor Gold Ale, lemon verbena, elderflower, meadowsweet and citrus fruits. Silver Bullet Gin uses the same botanicals as the original Wicked Wolf Gin, re-balanced to work at 57%. The Exmoor Vodka uses Sicilian lemons and is filtered through activated coconut charcoal.

Fordington Gin

Fordington, Dorchester
Distillery

ESSENTIAL INFORMATION
Key botanicals (Classic Fordington Gin):
   juniper, lemon balm, wormwood, mint,
   spices
Output: not disclosed
Location: 7 South Walks Rd, Dorchester
   DT1 1ED
Telephone: 07896 066982
Email: fordingtongin@gmail.com
Website: www.fordingtongin.co.uk
Facebook: www.facebook.com/
   fordingtongin
Instagram: @fordingtongin
Twitter: @fordingtongin

Opening hours:
Thursday-Friday 1000-1800
Saturday 1000-1600

Other reasons to go: Birthplace of Thomas Hardy, the Hardy Trail, Falconry park, Borough Gardens, Dorset Museum, Military Museum

Ros Nelmes, the brains behind Fordington Gin, drew on her wealth of knowledge and experience to create a twist on classic gin, starting on a Dorset kitchen table. She'd always loved gin, as well as distinctive food and drink, especially locally-grown and organic produce.

Ros's gins have won several gold medals, including the Taste of the West Awards; The China Wine and Spirits Awards; the International Women's Wine and Spirits Awards and The European Spirit Challenge, plus Silver at the World Gin Awards. It's also been shortlisted by Raymond Blanc.

The original Classic Fordington Gin is a true Dorset gem, handcrafted in small batches, combining juniper with star anise, wormwood and lemon balm. It's exceptionally smooth and sophisticated. Her Premium Gin combines juniper with blood orange.

Fordington also produces an imaginative range of seasonal gins, using local, organic and home-grown fruit and botanicals. In summer, they release their Orange and Elderflower Gin, made using local organic elderflower and blood oranges. The English Rose Gin is made with English rose petals, hibiscus and strawberry. The Rhubarb and Ginger Gin uses ginger from the Dorset Ginger Company and delicious, tart local rhubarb. In 2022 they made a Summer Pudding Gin for the Queen's Platinum Jubilee, and an exclusive Apple and Blackberry Gin.

Bespoke gins can be made for your special occasions on request.

G and Tea Distillers

Liskeard, Cornwall
Distillery

ESSENTIAL INFORMATION

Key botanicals (The Great Earl):
   Macedonian juniper, Spanish coriander,
   bitter orange, lemon peel, rose petals,
   bay leaves, apricot kernels

Output: not disclosed

Location: Liskeard, PL14 4LD (distilling
   with Colwith Farm Distillery, Lostwithiel)

Telephone: 07565 385278

Email: chris@gandtea.uk

Website: www.gandtea.uk

Facebook: www.facebook.com/gandtealtd

Instagram: @gandtealtd

Twitter: @gandtealtd

Opening hours: not open to the public

G and Tea Distillers were founded on a quest: to make a gin with a depth of flavour and smoothness that didn't rely on added flavourings.

With more than 14 years experience of tea blending, they set about infusing gins with their tea, then used the tea as a botanical in the distilling process. Working closely with Cornwall's only plough-to-bottle distillery, they created their original three gins, The Great Earl, a smokey citrus-forward gin (below); 80 Days (opposite, middle), a vibrant zesty London Dry with apple, pear, cinnamon and burnt orange; and Cornish Cream Tea Gin (opposite, top), packed with Cornish strawberry and apricot kernels for a creamy taste and texture while retaining a classic London dry style but with the bite of Sri Lankan black tea.

The tea blends are also available in their pure tea form, allowing everyone to enjoy the delicious tastes, whether its gin o'clock or not.

To their core range, they then added two seasonal blends: Winter Blend, packed with the spices, berries and aromas of winter; and the fruity Orchard and Berry Gin (opposite, bottom) with apple, blackcurrant and blueberry all grown within five miles of the distillery.

The Taste of the West Gold Award was given to the whole range, as well as Innovations National New Distiller of the Year and South West Boutique Drinks Brand of the Year. These were followed by a Great Taste award.

80 Days Gin has fast become the best-seller and biggest award-winner, with a vibrant and multi-layered flavour

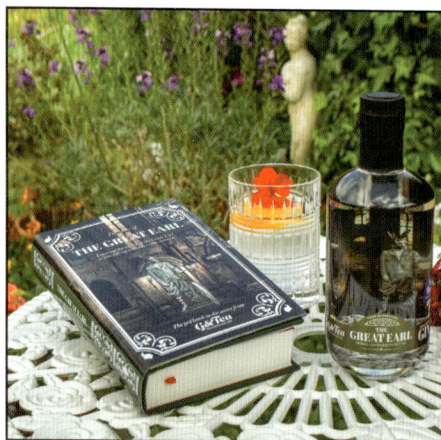

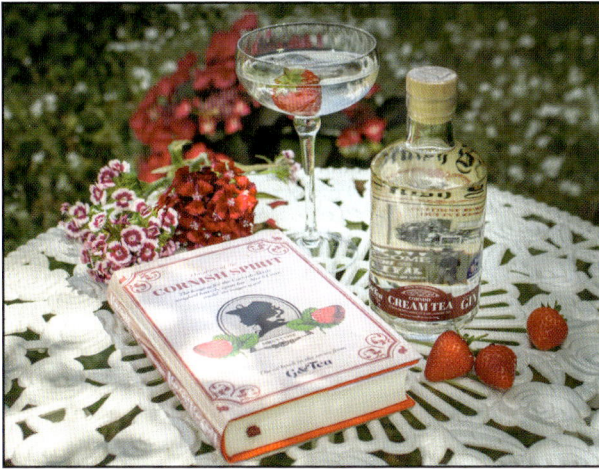

imparted by Cornish-grown apples and pears, spiciness from cinnamon and a well-rounded aftertaste from the caramelised burnt orange. It pairs perfectly with a light plain tonic and apple and pear slices. Alternatively, mix with blueberry and lime and add a kick of ginger beer to accentuate the grains of paradise. The result is a tropical taste, making it the perfect all-year-round gin.

Plymouth Gin

Plymouth, Devon
Distillery and bar

ESSENTIAL INFORMATION

Key botanicals (Plymouth Gin): juniper,
   coriander seed, green cardamom, lemon
   peel, orange peel

Output: 1,600,000+ bottles a year

Location: Black Friars Distillery, 60
   Southside Street, Plymouth, PL1 2LQ

Telephone: 01752 665292

Email: info@plymouthdistillery.com

Website: www.plymouthgin.com

Facebook: www.facebook.com/
   homeofplymouthgin

Instagram: @plymouthgin

Twitter: @plymouthgin

Opening hours:

Monday 1100-1630

Tuesday-Saturday 1100-1730

Sunday 1200-1700

Other reasons to go: The Barbican,
Smeaton's Tower, Bovisand Beach,
Pennywell Farm, National Marine Aquarium,
Plymouth Yacht Haven, The Mayflower Steps

Plymouth Gin (opposite, bottom), situated in Black Friars Distillery, is in the heart of Plymouth's picturesque waterfront, the Barbican. The cobbled narrow streets lead you past an array of independent shops, bars, cafes and art galleries as well as giving an insight into the area's rich historic past. A few minutes' walk from the distillery, which itself is only minutes outside of the city centre, you can see the Mayflower Steps, from where the Pilgrim Fathers set sail for the New World.

The Plymouth Gin Distillery claims to be England's oldest working gin distillery dating back to 1793. The waterfront was the perfect location because nearby Sutton Harbour was once Europe's largest spice port. Botanicals were always on hand, plus the good custom of the Royal Navy. Their gin had to be navy strength to ensure gun powder was still flammable if the gin happened to be spilt, as both items were stored next to each other on warships. Plymouth Gin is steeped in history but is now owned by Pernod Ricard who also have other successful brands such as Beefeater, Malfy and Monkey 47.

The distillery is open for tours daily with the exception of Christmas and new year. The Plymouth Gin Distillery Tour is available to book on the day, and features a one-hour tour of the site, a tasting of Plymouth Gin and two other Plymouth Gin products and a complimentary G&T (or miniature gin to take home) in the Refectory Bar. The gin cocktail bar is situated on the first floor. With advance booking, the Gin Connoisseur's Tour offers a more in-depth history and knowledge of gin as well as blind tastings. The Master Distiller's Tour offers this too, as well as the

opportunity for guests to make their own gin to take home. Other specialized tours, which must be pre-booked, include The Smeaton's Tower experience with Sean Harrison; Plymouth Gin Staycation; and The Foraging Tour.

Plymouth Gin itself is bottled at 41.2% and is made using seven botanicals. Plymouth Navy Strength Gin (opposite, left-hand bottle) is made with the same recipe, but is stronger at 57%. The distillery also makes Sloe Gin (opposite, right-hand bottle), Fruit Cup (a higher strength competitor to Pimms) as well as new ready-to-serve cocktails, Gin Martini and Gimlet (right).

Black and Gold Organic Distillery

Ponsanooth, Cornwall
Distillery

ESSENTIAL INFORMATION

Key botanicals (Original Organic Gin):
juniper, cubeb pepper, lemon peel, lime leaf, nutmeg
(Blood Orange Organic Gin) juniper, blood orange, pink grapefruit, pink peppercorn, lemon grass

Output: 5,000 bottles a year

Location: Ponsanooth, Cornwall TR3 7JQ

Telephone: 01872309270

Email: contact@blackandgolddistillery.co.uk

Website: blackandgolddistillery.co.uk

Facebook: www.facebook.com/
TheBlackAndGoldOrganicDistillery

Instagram: @blackandgoldorganicdistillery

Opening hours:
Monday-Sunday 0900-1700

Other reasons to go: Enys Gardens, Kennall Vale Nature Reserve, Falmouth

Black and Gold is a family-run distillery on a mission to create the smoothest, tastiest spirits in the industry, driven by a young team with innovative instincts.

They use a state-of-the-art still to achieve the smoothest spirit by extracting the purest part of the distillate.

The team's journey began in the summer of 2020, when they sat down to discuss how to extract the best flavours using techniques learned in other areas of mixology. They began with experimenting with a mini still, then upgraded to a big still to make larger batches. Once they were confident of the products, they tried them out on people all around Cornwall, then got them stocked by shops and local businesses all over the county.

Their Original Gin (below left), also known as their Cornish Dry, begins with a powerful burst of juniper followed by delicate citrus, spice and lime. To garnish, serve with a slice of lemon or lime.

The Blood Orange gin (right middle) is sweet, complemented by the tartness of grapefruit. It's a true summer gin, with a refreshing, crisp finish, and is best garnished with a slice of orange or pink grapefruit.

They recommend serving all the gins over ice with a quality tonic, as it doesn't take away from the flavour of the botanicals. Black and Gold gins generally cost £36.00 when this edition went to press.

Salcombe Gin and Salcombe Distilling Co.

Salcombe, Devon
Distillery, gin school and bar

ESSENTIAL INFORMATION

Key botanicals (Salcombe Gin): juniper, coriander seed, liquorice, cardamom, cubeb, lemon peel, lime peel, grapefruit peel, plus four secret ingredients

Output: not disclosed

Location: The Boathouse, 28 Island Street, Salcombe, TQ8 8DP

Telephone: 01548 288180

Email: ilovegin@salcombegin.com

Website: www.salcombegin.com

Facebook: www.facebook.com/SalcombeGin

Instagram: @salcombegin

Twitter: @SalcombeDCo

Opening hours:
Seasonal – see website for up-to-date information

Other reasons to go: Overbeck's Museum Home and Gardens, Salcombe North Sands, Mill Bay

Salcombe Gin was launched in 2016 by friends Howard Davies and Angus Lugsdin, who met in Salcombe while they were young sailing instructors in 1995. Angus in particular was intrigued by the art of distilling, so when they returned to Salcombe some years later, they decided to start Salcombe Distilling Company.

They spent 18 months developing their gin recipe and building The Boathouse (which houses the distillery), so called because it happens to be on the site of the boat repair yard that belonged to the sailing club where they met. They wanted the gin to be citrus led to link it to the history of the port – in the 19thC citrus cargo ships, called the Salcombe Fruiters, would carry oranges and lemons to Britain from overseas. They invited friends to take part in blind tastings until they found the perfect blend which they christened Salcombe Gin 'Start Point' (left).

Salcombe Distilling Co. uses the one-shot method (page 28). The still, named Provident (opposite, top left), is filled with English grain spirit, the botanicals and Dartmoor water, which is naturally soft, making a smooth gin. They also add the tails of the previous run in which is concentrated the earthy flavour of angelica

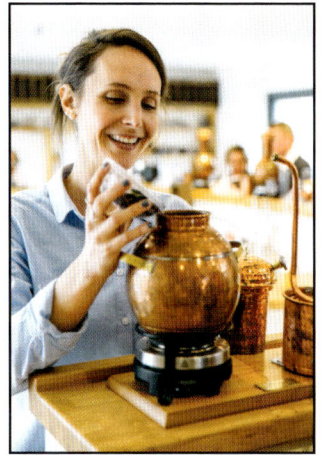

– a key element. The process takes around nine hours and produces enough spirit to fill 600 70-cl bottles. More Dartmoor water is added to bring it down to 44%.

Their flagship gin, Salcombe Gin 'Start Point', is best served on its own with ice, with a premium tonic water and a slice of red grapefruit, or in a Dry Martini with a twist of grapefruit peel. They also recommend mixing 25 ml of the gin with 25 ml of St Germain Elderflower Liqueur, 20 ml of freshly squeezed red grapefruit juice, 70 ml of chilled soda water and red grapefruit peel to make a St Clair cocktail.

In 2018, Salcombe Distilling Co. launched their Voyager Series limited edition gins made in collaboration with iconic winemakers and world renowned chefs. They also produce a cask-aged gin, Salcombe Gin 'Finisterre', in collaboration with Bodegas Tradición sherry house in Spain.

The distillery also has a bar (right) and hosts a Gin School (above right) where you develop and distil your own 70-cl bottle of gin and learn about the distillation process.

Salcombe Distilling Co. is one of the few distilleries that can be reached by boat. In 2018 they set up a service for delivering gin to visiting yachts in the South-west during the summer months.

Scilly Spirit Distillery

St Mary's Island, Isles of Scilly
Distillery, shop and gin school

ESSENTIAL INFORMATION

Key botanicals (Island Gin): juniper, cardamom, cassia bark, kaffir lime leaf, orange peel, fennel seed, pink peppercorns

Output: 12,000 bottles a year

Location: Old Town Lane, St Mary's, Isles of Scilly, TR21 0NN

Telephone: 01720 422400

Email: hello@scillyspirit.com

Website: www.scillyspirit.com

Facebook: www.facebook.com/scillyspirit

Instagram: @scillyspirit

Twitter: @scillyspirit

Opening hours:

Monday-Friday 0930-1630

Saturday 0930-1230

Distillery Tours: Tuesday 1530 and 1630
    Friday 1030 and 1130

Gin School: Tuesday 1130-1430
    Friday 1400-1700

Other reasons to go: Isles of Scilly archipelago, boat trip to Bishop Rock Lighthouse, beaches, rare wildlife species, local artists, galleries, restaurants, hotels

At the most south-westerly point of the UK, husband and wife team Arthur and Hilary Miller established their Scilly Spirit Distillery on St Mary's Island in the enchanting Isles of Scilly. The distillery opened May 2019, and they were quickly receiving many impressive awards within weeks of releasing their Island Gin.

When they were developing their brand, the inspiration for their Island Gin (below) stemmed from an event way back on 18th January 1665, when a spice trade ship was wrecked off their local Bishop Rock, carrying peppercorns from Java. Peppercorns therefore feature as a key botanical.

The outstanding beauty of the Isles of Scilly and its seaside heritage provided founders Arthur and Hilary with a rich territory to inspire their bottle design. They pay homage to the lighthouse which stands on Bishop Rock through the bottle's shape, and the aqua-green colour captures the Scilly seas and uses imagery of the local Western Rocks. Even their tamper seal was designed as a reference to the pilot gig boats, a key part of Scilly's heritage.

They launched a Navy Strength Gin in November 2020, naming it Atlantic Strength (opposite, top left, left bottle), because Arthur and Hilary hand pick the wild Atlantic fennel which grows along the island's coastline. In October 2021, they released their Rosé aged gin (opposite, top right) which is barrel-aged in former port casks to deliver the tawny rose colour, with a hint of dry vermouth on the palate. They worked with artist Oriel Hicks from a local gallery to replicate her glass work of the sunset over Samson for the label on the back of the clear Rosé Island Gin 50-cl bottles. View it through the bottle and you'll experience a rosy good-weather gin sunset.

Design excellence aside, the gin itself was awarded Gold at the 2022 International Wine and Spirit Challenge – one of only 16 UK distillers to receive such an award from the 1,200 gins entered.

The duo still complete every aspect of making their three Island Gins: from the small-batch distillation runs to bottling and labelling, packing and dispatch of website orders. Not to mention fulfilling all trade shipments, loading their gins on to the thrice-weekly freight ship to Penzance.

These local, authentic, artisan gins showcase their owners' total commitment. Try their Island Gins in person, an excuse to enjoy the beautiful Isles of Scilly while you sip.

Silent Pool Distillers

Aldbury, Surrey
Distillery

ESSENTIAL INFORMATION

Key botanicals (Silent Pool Gin): juniper, coriander, grains of paradise, lime, sweet orange, bitter orange, kaffir lime leaf, elderflower, lavender, chamomile, linden flower, rose petal, fresh and dried peat
(Silent Pool Rare Citrus Gin): juniper, Buddha's hand, Natsu Dai Dai, Hirado Buntan, green Seville orange, coriander, timur pepper, wild forest pepper, kampot, voatsiperifery pepper
Output: 800,000 bottles a year
Location: Shere Road, Albury, GU5 9BW
Telephone: 01483 229136
Email: office@silentpooldistillers.com
Website: www.silentpooldistillers.com
Facebook: www.facebook.com/ SilentPoolGin
Instagram: @silentpoolgin
Twitter: @SilentPoolGin

Opening hours:
Monday-Friday 1000-1700
Saturday 1000-1800
Sunday 1000-1600

Other reasons to go: On-site bar and tours, Surrey Hills

Nestled in the heart of the Surrey Hills, on The Duke of Northumberland's estate on the banks of the legendary Silent Pool, you'll find the Silent Pool Distillery. It was set up in 2014 by a pair of Surrey locals with the grand vision to produce handcrafted artisan spirits in a sustainable distillery adjacent to the ancient water source known as Silent Pool. Whilst all the products have their own distinctive taste, each is united by Silent Pool's shared purpose and vision. The distillers are dedicated to crafting recipes which are a symphony of flavours; each ingredient is complementary without dominating the palate. From distillation to bottling, everything is done on-site. The team is comprised of 35 full-time staff members who oversee every detail of production. Silent Pool Gin is now exported to over 45 countries, with the ethos of the brand unchanged; creating luxury spirits from the finest botanicals using sustainable methods.

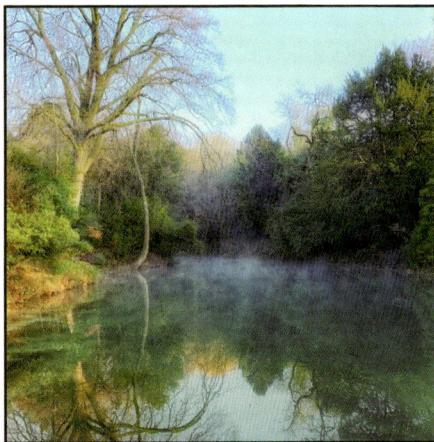

Animal Spirits

Bermondsey, London
Craft producer

ESSENTIAL INFORMATION
Key botanicals (The Rabbit Gin): juniper,
    cardamom, orange peel, magnolia berries,
    mint, Kazbek hops, Sichuan green pepper,
    two secret botanicals, corn spirit
Output: 1,000 bottles a year
Location: 34 Raymouth Rd, London SE16
    2DB
Telephone: not disclosed
Email: info@animal-spirits.com
Website: www.animal-spirits.com
Facebook: www.facebook.com/
    WeAreAnimalSpirits
Instagram: @weareanimalspirits

Opening hours: not open to the public

Animal Spirits is a small Bermondsey-based craft producer. Their brand is all about capturing, unleashing and celebrating the animal kingdom, whilst upholding their commitment to a strong sustainability ethos. They unite science and nature through co-founder Dr Lukas Radosa's background in microbiology. Eva Liparova is their other co-founder, with a background in theatre production and product development.

The Rabbit Gin (below left and next page, bottom) is Animal Spirits' first product, launched in November 2020. As the UK's only corn-based London Dry, Rabbit Spirit is distilled with premium corn spirit, responsibly-sourced organic juniper from the Białowieca Forest in Poland and nine unusual botanicals such as cardamom, Kazbek hops, Sichuan green pepper and magnolia berry, as well as two secret ingredients used in natural medicine as aphrodisiacs – a nod to one of the rabbit's favourite activities.

Thanks to Lukas' knowledge of natural products, each botanical tells its story on the nose, palate and finish. The Sichuan green pepper is both electrifying and numbs the tip of your tongue, then gives a spicy, warming sensation. The buttery corn spirit balances the spicy flavours with hints of butterscotch and popcorn. Thanks to its higher viscosity, the gin has a luscious, 'oily' mouthfeel and texture. At 44% ABV the Rabbit Gin is surprisingly smooth and makes a great Martini. The gin is distilled and bottled at their London-based distillery partner Thames Distillers, where they use a single pot distillation of diluted corn spirit and botanicals without prolonged maceration – only the finest distillate is

collected. It is then blended with premium corn spirit at a secret ratio before diluting it down to 44% ABV with the purest spring water. The Rabbit Gin sits in the bottle for another three months to round up the taste before it is released for sale.

The Rabbit Gin is available to buy on their website, shipping in plastic-free packaging, or you can order it at various bars in and around Bermondsey Street and the Bermondsey Beer Mile.

Jensen's Gin and Bermondsey Distillery

Bermondsey, London

Distillery

ESSENTIAL INFORMATION

Key botanicals (Jensen's Bermondsey Dry): juniper, coriander seed, dried lemon and orange

Output: 50,000 bottles a year

Location: 55 Stanworth Street, London SE1 3NY

Telephone: 02072 371500

Email: info@bermondseygin.com

Website: www.bermondseygin.com

Facebook: www.facebook.com/jensengin

Instagram: @jensensgin

Twitter: @jensensgin

Opening hours:

Monday-Sunday 1100-1700

Tours on Wednesdays and Thursdays, booking essential

Other reasons to go: Druid Street Market, HMS Belfast, Maltby Street Market, White Cube Bermondsey, The Scoop, Fashion and Textile Museum

When Christian Jensen first tasted vintage gins from London's lost distilleries, he began a journey. Creating a finely-balanced gin that honoured these forgotten recipes became his obsession. As a result, Jensen's is distilled in small batches, using only traditional gin botanicals. There's really nothing new about that, which is why Jensen's is different. Distilled in Bermondsey, London, it is gin as it was, and gin as it should be.

The London Dry (left bottle) is citrus-led and the smooth feel in the mouth means it is great as a sipping drink or in a Dry Martini. The Old Tom (right bottle) is more punchy, as it has more juniper, spice and plenty of liquorice. Jensen's also produces seasonal gins.

You can do an after-hours tour of the distillery, where you can learn about distilling, the Jensen's brand and London's gin history. This is followed by a tutored tasting session and cocktail masterclass, including a G&T on arrival.

Brighton Gin

Brighton and Hove
Distillery

ESSENTIAL INFORMATION
**Key botanicals (Brighton Gin): juniper,
coriander seed, fresh orange zest, fresh
lime zest, milk thistle seed**
Output: circa 25,000 bottles a year
**Location: 35A Vale Rd, Portslade, Brighton
and Hove**
Telephone: 012734 48092
Email: cheers@brightongin.com
Website: www.brightongin.com
Facebook: www.facebook.com/BrightonGin
Instagram: @brightonginstergram
Twitter: @BrightonGin

Opening hours:
Monday-Friday 0900-1700
**Distillery tours from 1530 on selected
Saturdays, booking essential**

**Other reasons to go: Brighton Beach,
Brighton Pavilion**

Brighton Gin was founded by Kathy Caton, developed at her kitchen table ten years ago, and epitomises the spirit of Brighton: unusual, fun-loving, open-minded, fiercely independent and ethically-conscious. Based at the city's first legal distillery, the small team of friends and family produce award-winning gin a stone's throw from the sea. Every bottle of Brighton Gin is filled, wax-sealed and labelled by hand. It claims to be the UK's first vegan certified gin, including the packaging, label gum and wax top.

The classic Brighton Gin Pavilion Strength (top left) is priced at £39 and is a super smooth London Dry, best served with a light tonic and a slice of orange to enhance the fresh citrus botanicals and the gin's subtle sweetness. The colour of the label and wax seal is that of Brighton's iconic seafront railings.

Brighton Gin Seaside Strength (below left) is priced at £49, and is a navy strength gin loaded with four times the juniper and double all other botanicals of the original Pavilion Strength. While juniper is the star, the Seaside Strength also combines hints of candied orange with pine and spice. It makes for a brilliant G&T when garnished with a wheel of lime. In 2021 Brighton Gin launched ready-to-serve canned drinks, a Raspberry Crush and a Lemon Verbena Garden Collins. Made from natural ingredients and in endlessly recyclable packaging, they make for the perfect sundowner on the beach, or anywhere else for that matter.

Canova Gin and Canova Hall

Brixton, London
Distillery and bar

ESSENTIAL INFORMATION

Key botanicals (Canova Gin): juniper, coriander seed, liquorice root, lemon peel, orange peel, goji berry, apple, pear, rosehip

Output: not disclosed

Location: 250 Ferndale Road, Brixton, London, SW9 8BQ

Telephone: 020 7733 8356

Email: bookings@canovahall.com

Website: www.canovahall.com

Facebook: www.facebook.com/CanovaHall

Instagram: @canovahall

Twitter: @canovahall

Opening hours:

Monday-Thursday 0800-0000

Friday 0800-0200

Saturday 0900-0200

Sunday 0900-2300

Other reasons to go:

Brixton Village, Brixton Academy, Hootananny

The Albion & East bar group opened Canova Hall, their second bar and microdistillery, in September 2017 in the former worker's hall of Le Bon Marché – which was Britain's first department store. It is a glorious building with charming outdoor seating. The two floors offer hot-desk facilities (including bottomless coffee from £10); freshly-made pizza from their wood-burning oven during the day; cocktails and dinner in the evening; and bottomless brunch on the weekends – for £30 you get brunch and unlimited drinks for two hours.

Canova Hall offers the same gin experiences as its sister bar Martello Hall, bringing the Hackney bar's warehouse glamour to trendy Brixton, with exposed ceilings and plaster walls, a tiled bar and wooden benches. They make their own Canova Gin in their still, Grace, sited under the DJ booth, which they serve with Mediterranean tonic, Creme de Mure, blackberries and lemon. Martello Gin is also served here, alongside Jensen's Old Tom (page 55), East London Liquor Company Batch 2, and Aviation.

The gin is served on a cocktail trolley, which carries various garnishes and tonics from which you make your own perfect serve. You can also 'Book a Bartender' who will mix cocktails at your table.

Chilgrove Gin and Chilgrove Spirits

Chichester, West Sussex
Distillery and gin school

ESSENTIAL INFORMATION

Key botanicals (Chilgrove Signature Edition Gin): juniper, coriander seed, liquorice root, grains of paradise, lime, orange, bitter orange, wild water mint, savory

Output: 50,000 bottles a year

Location: The Bakery, Watergate, Chichester, PO19 9RJ

Telephone: 02392 631808

Email: info@chilgrovespirits.com

Website: www.chilgrovespirits.com

Facebook: www.facebook.com/chilgrove

Instagram: @chilgrovespirits

Twitter: @ChilgroveGin

Opening hours:
Booking essential for Chilgrove Gin School

Other reasons to go:
Fishbourne Roman Palace, Chichester Cathedral, Pallant House Gallery

Chilgrove Spirits claim to be the only distillers in the UK to make their gin from a 100 per cent grape-alcohol base as opposed to the more common cereal base – and are still the only distillery still using 100 per cent grape alcohol. The operation is run by Christopher Beaumont-Hutchings and Celia (below) who grew up in Holland – the home of gin. Traditionally, genever (Dutch gin) was made using alcohol distilled from wine, but because the Little Ice Age (14th to 19th centuries) caused a wine shortage in Europe, many distillers turned to a cereal base. Given Celia's Dutch heritage and their own taste preferences, it made sense to revive the grape base. In grape spirit, botanicals act differently – the grape emphasises the floral flavours in the gin – so they spent a few months of trial and error to find the right balance of flavours to complement the spirit, with the help of Charles Maxwell at Thames Distillery.

Chilgrove recommends adding two shots of its Signature Edition Gin (left) to tonic water, with plenty of ice and a sprig of fresh English mint. It also works well in a gin fizz cocktail: mix equal measures of the gin, fresh pink grapefruit juice and fresh lemon juice and top up with English sparkling wine (or champagne or prosecco if you prefer), adding a twist of orange peel to garnish.

They also produce Chilgrove Bluewater Edition Gin (opposite, top left), a London Dry which is bottled at 46% and takes inspiration from the relationship between Australia and England by incorporating native botanicals from both countries: finger limes, lemon myrtle, riberry and Davidson plum from Australia and mint, savory, angelica and coriander from England. These botanicals are illustrated on the sides of the bottle and are distilled with the grape-alcohol base plus

water from the South Downs. The blue neck of the bottle is a reference to Captain James Cook (the first European to map the coastline of New Zealand and land on Australia's east coast at Botany Bay) and his first voyage on the HM Bark Endeavour. The name Bluewater refers to deep water (ocean) sailing.

They also make Chilgrove Bramble Edition Gin (top right), which includes all the botanicals of the London Dry plus English blackberries, which are infused in the spirit to create a deep, ruby red colour. They recommend serving 50 ml of the Bramble Edition with 100 ml of light tonic, plenty of ice and a frozen blackberry and slices of apple to garnish.

The Chilgrove Gin School (middle right) is held at The White Horse in Chilgrove. You get a brief history of gin while sipping a Chilgrove G&T, followed by a talk on how the company operates. But the main event is the interactive cocktail making masterclass, typically involving four or five different serves.

Contact info@chilgrovespirits.com to book. The masterclasses can be held on any day of the week and at alternative venues by arrangement. They can be tailored for groups of two to a hundred people and can be combined as a package with dinner and accommodation at The White Horse.

Future plans include a locally-produced ice cream and a Chilgrove Vodka sorbet.

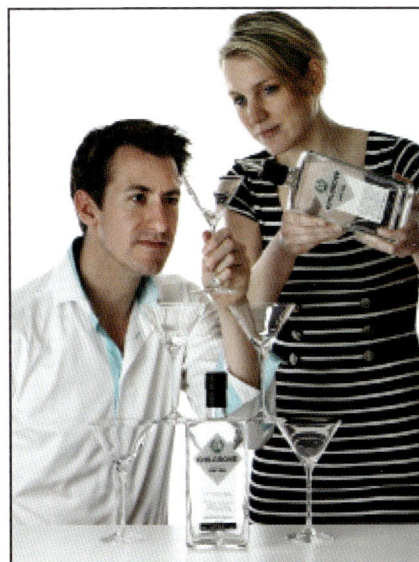

Levin Down Goodwood Gin

Chichester, West Sussex
Distillery and shop

ESSENTIAL INFORMATION

Key botanicals (Levin Down Goodwood Gin): juniper, coriander, mint, gorse flower

Output: not disclosed

Location: The Goodwood Estate, Chichester, West Sussex, PO18 0PX

Telephone: 01243 755000

Email: farmfood@goodwood.com

Website: www.goodwood.com

Facebook: www.facebook.com/ GoodwoodEstate

Instagram: @goodwood

Opening hours:
Goodwood Farm Shop
Monday-Friday 0900-1700
Saturday 0900-1500

Other reasons to go: The Goodwood Hotel, Afternoon Tea and Tour at Goodwood House, Festival of Speed, Goodwood Revival, Glorious Goodwood

Levin Down Goodwood Gin (left) is a small-batch London Dry which reflects the agricultural heritage of the 11,000-acre Goodwood Estate (bottom left).

Goodwood is the ancestral home of the Dukes of Richmond and Gordon, who has been closely involved in the creation of the gin.

Too steep for the plough and abundant in English Juniper, Levin Down, derived from 'Leave-Alone-Hill' is an ancient hill on the Goodwood Estate. It was here that the Charlton Hunt earned fame, drawing the nobility and gentry of the 18thC to Goodwood. Among them was the third Duke of Devonshire, who galloped his horse down Levin Down at such a pace that he flew over a five-barred gate at the bottom. This daring feat introduced fence jumping to the hunt.

With a character shaped by the wild-grown botanicals sourced from the estate, Levin Down Goodwood Gin is handcrafted using traditional methods, and distilled with mineral water naturally chalk-filtered through the South Downs. The result is an authentic London Dry from the wilds of West Sussex – luxurious and soft on the nose and balanced on the palate. Native gorse flower gives it a tantalising hint of warm toasted coconut and vanilla, moving on to zesty citrus and characteristic juniper.

Levin Down Goodwood Gin was awarded London Dry Gold, Contemporary Gold and Ultra-Premium Silver at The Gin Masters 2022 blind tasting from more than 500 entries. It is bottled at 43.6% ABV and available to buy at Goodwood Farm Shop and online from Goodwood.com at £40 for a 70 cl bottle.

The Gin Kitchen

Dorking, Surrey
Distillery, bar, restaurant and shop

ESSENTIAL INFORMATION

Key botanicals (Dancing Dragontail Summer Gin): wild Kossovo juniper, green cardamom, cassia bark, pink grapefruit zest
Output: not disclosed
Location: Punchbowl Lane, Dorking, RH5 4DX
Telephone: 01306 889598
Email: fabulous@gin.kitchen
Website: www.gin.kitchen
Facebook: www.facebook.com/theginkitchen
Instagram: @theginkitchen
Twitter: @theginkitchen

Opening hours:
Vary with the seasons, check website

Other reasons to go: Box Hill, Denbies Hillside, Leith Hill, The Deepdene Trail, Dorking Museum and Heritage Centre

Co-founder Kate was working as an aeronautical engineer. On her way to the airport to catch a flight to Paris, she heard a radio story about craft gin-making. Instantly inspired, she called her best friend Helen and announced they should start their own distillery. Helen was immediately on board, and the two women teamed up with one simple plan: to create the finest gin possible. So, the Gin Kitchen was born. Initially started in a coal shed in the garden of a local pub, word started spreading about their artisan spirits, and within mere months the Gin Kitchen was making waves from Cumbria to Cornwall. As the business expanded, so did the team and premises – in 2018 they moved into 170 year-old farm buildings, which are now home to their growing business.

Handcrafted with the finest botanicals from around the globe, the Gin Kitchen's range comprises five ultra-premium gins.

The refreshingly floral Dancing Dragontail Summer Gin (next page, middle right) boasts a strong citrus taste from pink grapefruit, and a kick of aromatic green cardamom. Their Insane Ostrich Classic Gin (next page, bottom left) offers an adventurous, sweet scent from piney juniper balanced with zest and a little pepper, ideal for making a delicious martini. Blushing Monkey Pink Gin (next page, second from left), with a delightful yet subtly sweet twist, blushes to a pearly pink with the addition of tonic. The Ginger Cat Gin (next page, second from right) boasts silky smooth tonka from South America, Iranian orange flowers, cinnamon, orange zest and ginger. Full-bodied, rich and smooth, Gutsy Monkey Winter Gin

(bottom right) showcases subtle citrus with a complex aromatic flavour for a bold and spicy spirit.

Found in luxury stores (including Fortnum & Mason), five-star hotels, Michelin-starred restaurants, specialist merchants, bars, and exported to three continents, Gin Kitchen spirits can also be purchased online and in the on-site gin shop next to the Dorking-based distillery. Alongside the distillery and gin shop, the Gin Kitchen has two exceptional cocktail bars offering G&Ts and creative cocktails – the stylish Orangery Bar, and the rustic Calf Shed, where an acclaimed tapas menu is also served. Guests can learn more about the Gin Kitchen collection with a Gin Tasting & Distillery Tour Experience, Cocktail Masterclass or Gin Distilling Experience. A popular bottomless brunch is also served at weekends.

58 and Co.

Haggerston, London
Distillery and gin school

ESSENTIAL INFORMATION

Key botanicals (58 and Co. London Dry
    Gin): juniper, coriander seed, cubeb
    pepper, Egyptian lemon, bergamot, pink
    grapefruit, vanilla
Output: not disclosed
Location: 329 Acton Mews, London, E8 4EF
Telephone: 020 3095 9734
Email: carmen@58andco.com
Website: www.58andco.com
Facebook: www.facebook.com/58andco
Instagram: @58andco
Twitter: @58andco

Opening hours:
Distillery
    Monday-Friday 0930-1730
Gin School
    Friday 1830-2130
    Saturday 1400-1700

Other reasons to go: Broadway Market,
Columbia Road Flower Market, Hackney

Carmen O'Neal, the founder, says 'we make it easy to feel wonderful about your drink because 58 and Co. is guaranteed to be exceptional every time. By drinking us, you're helping support people and planet'.

She mixes 'traditional distilling methods with progressive ideas' to give you 'an elevated drinking experience' and collaborates with other businesses on food waste reduction and sustainable distilling. A confident pitch, aimed at the consciences of a young market which likes to have a few drinks without getting bogged down with the state of the planet. Waste products from the distilling go back to Loddington Farm, a partner of 58 and Co., to make compost for the apple trees and juniper bushes Carmen has planted, and whose fruit finds its way back into bottles of 58 and Co. gin.

Reviews back up her claims: 'bold, rich and creamy, this gin offers up a smorgasbord of juniper, mint and sugary lemon zest... an exquisitely balanced example of what the most refined spirit elixir can deliver' (from the IWSC 2020 tasting notes).

The distillery's trendy East End location in Haggerston Mews is next to the overground station and Haggerston Arches, an impressive space which 58 and Co. hire out for events and private parties, and makes a great setting for its gin school.

The signature London Dry (left) remains the distillery's core offering, with the Apple and Hibiscus Prink Gin also becoming very popular. It makes a refreshing moreish cocktail: the 58 Cosmo. Mix one part lime, two parts cranberry juice, two parts Cointreau or Triple Sec with four parts Apple and Hibiscus Gin. Serve in a martini glass with a twist of orange peel.

Sacred Gin and Sacred Spirits Company

Highgate, London
Distillery

ESSENTIAL INFORMATION
Key botanicals (Sacred Gin): juniper, coriander, liquorice, cardamom, cinnamon, lemon, lime, orange, pink grapefruit, nutmeg, frankincense
Output: 70,000 bottles a year
Location: Highgate High Street, London, N6 5HX
Telephone: 020 8340 2817
Email: info@sacredgin.com
Website: www.sacredgin.com
Facebook: www.facebook.com/SacredSpiritsCompany
Instagram: @sacredgin
Twitter: @SacredGin

Opening hours:
Tuesday-Friday 1100-1830
Saturday 1030-1830
Sunday 1100-1730

Other reasons to go: The original 'Make Your Own Gin' experience, distillery visit and tastings, North London attractions

Ian Hart and Hilary Whitney founded Sacred Spirits in 2008 at their house in Highgate. As a child, he was intrigued by the process of distilling, and when he was old enough a G&T became his drink of choice. He'd often thought about creating his own London Dry, liking the idea of "producing what is traditionally a London product, actually in London."

Ian has a degree in Natural Sciences, and worked for many years in finance. With the crash of 2008, work became scarce and Ian was drawn back to his scientific roots. He experimented with extracting water from below-par vintages to create a better quality wine, then turned to gin.

Ian believes he is the first to use the vacuum distillation method to make gin, rather than the traditional pot still. The vacuum creates a lower boiling point: the botanicals aren't 'cooked', but their essence gently drawn out. Ian designed the stills (left) himself, giving him complete control over the production process and allowing him to adapt the equipment to suit each distillation.

Each of the botanicals used in Sacred Gin is macerated in English wheat spirit for four to six weeks to allow for optimum extraction. The distillates are then distilled separately, to allow for experimentation with different flavour combinations, before blending them for the gin. One of the more unusual botanicals used in their signature London Dry is *Boswellia sacra* (Latin for Frankincense), which inspired the name Sacred Gin and gives the gin a fresh, resinous flavour.

Ian likes Sacred Gin in a Dry Martini made with Sacred English Dry Vermouth, and Hilary recommends serving the gin in a

Gimlet with Rose's Lime Cordial.

In the early days, Ian and Hilary would take their gins into the local pub for the regulars to taste. The 23rd recipe was their lucky number – everyone knew this was the winner. The pub's landlord agreed to sell the spirit behind the bar, a nice incentive to produce the first 2,500 bottles.

Encouraged by the success of Sacred Gin, Ian also added to the range a Sacred Old Tom Gin (winner of The World's Best Old Tom Gin – top left bottle), a bespoke gin for Tate galleries, Sacred Organic Sloe Gin, Sacred Christmas Pudding Gin, plus several botanical gins such as Sacred Cardamom Gin (top, right bottle) and Sacred Pink Grapefruit Gin (right middle).

Over the years, Sacred has developed a knack for rejuvenating the neglected. Sacred produced the first English vermouths (right), two of which have won World's Best awards, and Sacred Orange Whiskey Liqueur – described as "an Old Fashioned in a bottle". They also produce Sacred Organic Vodka, Sacred Rosehip Cup (an English alternative to Campari), Sacred Peated English Whiskey, and much more. The full complement can be seen on their website. In 2022, the distillery moved premises to Highgate High Street, adding a bottle shop and tasting room, with an additional shop near Spitalfields Market.

Jim and Tonic

London
Distillery and mobile bars

ESSENTIAL INFORMATION
Key botanicals (Mediterranean Gin):
   juniper, coriander, fresh rosemary,
   thyme, basil grown at London sites using
   urban farming techniques
Output: not disclosed
Location: Print House at Jim & Co.
133 High St, London E15 2RB
   Bar locations: Elephant and Castle,
   Mayfair and Brixton Village
Telephone: 020 3984 9887
Email: hello@jimandtonic.com
Website: www.jimandtonic.com
Facebook: www.facebook.com/
   jimandtonicdistillery
Instagram: @jimandtonicdistillery
Twitter: @jimandtonicltd

Opening hours:
Bar hours vary

Other reasons to go: London attractions

Jim writes: Move over Gordon, Jim is in town. That's me, Jim, the founder and CEO of Jim and Tonic. As a small, independent gin company every customer genuinely makes a difference to us and we hope you'll end up visiting one of our bars or ordering some gin online (or both) so we can get to know each other some more.

I've always been partial to a G&T, even when it was unfashionable and something your Gran would drink.

My lightbulb moment came, randomly, in 2016 when I was on a ski trip in Norway and the bars there were serving these unbelievable gins in big balloon glasses, with loads of different brands, tonics and epic garnishes. It wasn't really a thing back in the UK in 2016 (most pubs would serve a Gordon's with rubbish tonic, no ice and a scabby bit of lemon) so I decided to create Jim and Tonic.

What started out as me and my friends serving craft gins out of my converted vintage van (opposite, middle) has grown into a network of gin bars, an online shop and a distillery focussed on another passion of mine: sustainability and eco-practices.

We distil four core-range gins, as well as limited editions. And we have a grand plans for producing our own range of rums, vodka, whisky and other spirits soon, so watch this space.

The Mediterranean Gin (left) uses fresh basil grown in London. Our Rhubarb Gin (opposite, bottom right) has fresh rhubarb and locally-sourced honey. Our Grapefruit Gin (opposite, top right) uses grapefruit peel and citra hops; and our London Dry Gin (opposite, top left) uses local London apples and linen blossom.

Branding themselves as a sustainable urban gin distillery, they either grow their own botanicals or source them from local suppliers in the London area, including community gardens. Other notable achievements are their eco-friendly packaging and light bottles to reduce carbon emissions when transporting their products.

In August 2022, Jim and Tonic launched at The Print House in Stratford, East London. See more details in their Gin Spotlight on page 210 of this guide.

The Green Room Distillery

London
Distillery

ESSENTIAL INFORMATION
Key botanicals (Green Room Gin): juniper, cinnamon, cloves, grains of paradise, fresh pink grapefruit, orange, lime
Output: 1,500 bottles a year
Location: Behind the Scenes, London
Telephone: 07751905812
Email: hello@greenroomdistillery.com
Website: www.greenroomdistillery.com
Facebook: www.facebook.com/greenroomdistillery
Instagram: @greenroomdistillery
Twitter: @greenroomgin

Opening hours: not open to the public

The multi-awarding winning Green Room Distillery was started in 2020 by two friends (opposite, top right) from the world of theatre. When the pandemic hit and stage doors closed, they turned to distilling. Their unique, small-batch spirits include Green Room Gin, Houselight Gin, Flyman's Strength Gin, Sloe Gin and Triple Filtered Vodka, all distilled, hand-filled, labelled and finished with a wax seal behind the scenes in London.

The distillery is based in what used to be the distillers' design studio: the servers have been replaced with stills, and the network cables with tubing. They run a traditional 40-litre pot still called Guinevere for all of their gins, and a 25-litre column still for their vodka.

Green Room are proud to have partnered with the entertainment charity, Backup. For every bottle of gin, vodka or sloe gin that they sell, Green Room donate £1 to Backup.

The premium Green Room Gin was recently crowned Winner at The Gin Guide Awards 2022, and Silver at the 2022 World Gin Awards, International Spirits Challenge and London Spirits Competition. Each batch consists of only 42 bottles, distilled with 14 botanicals to create its unique flavour, including fresh orange, pink grapefruit, lime, grains of paradise, cloves and cinnamon.

Flyman's Strength Gin (opposite, bottom) is their Navy-style product, bottled at 57%. It is called Flyman's as a nod to the 'flymen' in theatres, who work high above the stage, hauling the scenery in and out of view. It is perfect for cocktails, especially a Gimlet. It recently took home Two Stars at the Great Taste Awards 2022.

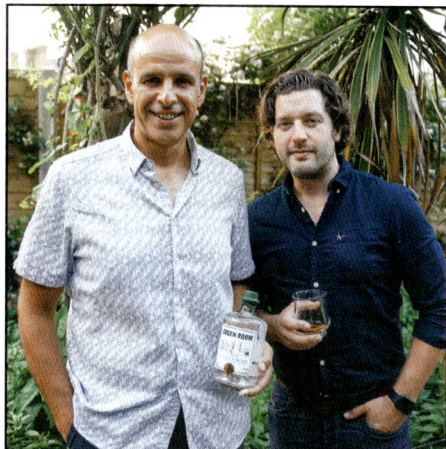

Also winning One Star at the Great Taste Awards 2022, Green Room's Sloe Gin (above) is steeped with hand-picked sloes from Somerset. Homemade sugar syrup is added at the end of the process to achieve its nice balance of sweetness.

Finally, the award-winning Triple Filtered Vodka (middle) is made from Green Room's own sugar-based mash, fermented for two weeks, distilled six times, and triple-filtered through charcoal to deliver a unique sweet and smooth taste, to be bottled at 45%.

In 2022, Green Room partnered with Trinity, a London Michelin-starred restaurant, to create their own seasonal gins. These four unique distillations are used throughout the year to pair with Trinity's seasonal menus. They also collaborate with Bacchus and Brodie and chef Josh Dalloway to host the No.9 Supper Club, featuring a unique Green Room Gin cocktail and five-course tasting menu. Places can be booked on their website.

The distillery is run by two professionals who would usually be working behind the scenes, so they prefer to remain nameless and let the gin do the talking.

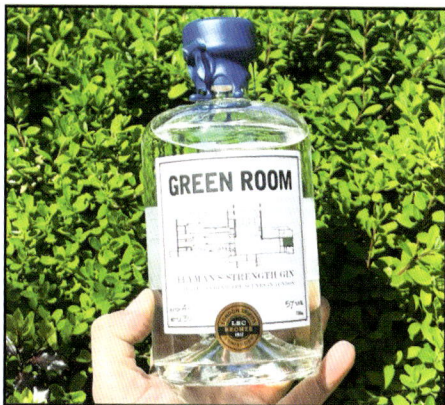

Anno Distillers

Marden, Kent
Distillery

ESSENTIAL INFORMATION

Key botanicals (Anno Kent Dry Gin): juniper, lavender, chamomile, hop, samphire **(Extreme 95):** juniper, coriander, liqourice, cassia bark, eucalyptus, grapefruit, Kentish hops, fennel, nutmeg

Output: 50,000 bottles a year

Location: Unit 4, Crest Industrial Estate, Pattenden Lane, Marden, TN12 9QJ

Telephone: 01622 833278

Email: info@annodistillers.co.uk

Website: www.annodistillers.co.uk

Facebook: www.facebook.com/ AnnoDistillers

Instagram: @annodistillers

Twitter: @annodistillers

Opening hours:
Monday-Friday 0900-1700

Other reasons to go: Tonbridge Castle, Leeds Castle, Haysden Country Park, The Hop Farm, wineries (Chapel Down, Hush Heath)

Anno's subtitle 'The spirit of alchemy' is a nice promotional tag, but this well-established craft gin distillery is a far cry from the medieval alchemist with his reputation as a charlatan.

However, just as medieval alchemists were on a quest to convert base metals into gold, the founders of Anno, Andy Reason and Norman Lewis (now retired), manage to turn simple ingredients into excellent gin. Both have PhDs in science and worked for GlaxoSmithKline before venturing out on their own in 2011, as early pioneers of the craft gin craze.

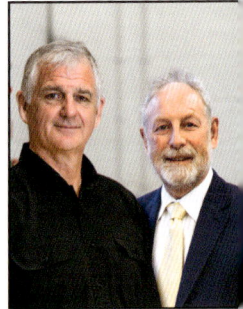

Their hallmark is consistent quality; their expertise helped them achieve worldwide acclaim in 2020 with the creation of the aptly-named Extreme 95 – a 95% ABV gin, which proudly boasts the title of 'the world's strongest gin' (see page 30 for a Gin Spotlight). Their flagship gin, Anno Kent Dry Gin (left), is a smooth, complex, floral gin, good for sipping and mixing, and can claim to be 'the taste of Kent'. Hops are a Kentish crop, and so is the samphire which grows on the coastal saltmarshes and gives a sweet, grassy dimension to the gin along with Kentish florals.

The distillery itself is tucked away in Marden, Kent, on a small industrial estate. While its exterior may not be as attractive as others in this guide, the distillery hosts tours and tastings to educate your palate in a comfortable air-conditioned room

with space for 24 visitors. After a tour of the distilling area, you will be guided by a member of the Anno team to enjoy a tasting of the Anno range, paired with a range of mixers and garnishes, with generous portions. For those who want to test their own alchemy skills, Anno also run a blending experience where guests can create their own gin concoctions to be bottled, personalised and taken home.

Anno were also creators of Kent's first whisky, and their portfolio now includes rums. Some favourites include Orange and Honey Gin, Berry Pink Gin (bottom right), Sloe Gin and a Blueberry and Strawberry 'Magic' Colour-Changing Gin that would make medieval alchemists proud.

The Old Bakery Gin, Rum and Whisky Distillery

Palmers Green, London
Distillery and pop up bar

ESSENTIAL INFORMATION

Key botanicals (Old Bakery Gin): juniper, plus three secret ingredients
Output: 300 bottles a week
Location: The Old Grain Store, 4 Pymmes Mews, London, N13 4PF
Telephone: 020 8829 8241
Email: hello@oldbakerygin.com
Website: www.oldbakerygin.com
Facebook: www.facebook.com/oldbakerygin
Instagram: @oldbakerygin

Opening hours:
Distillery
    Monday-Friday 0900-1700
Pop-up bar
    Last Saturday of every month 1600-2300

Other reasons to go: Broomfield Park, Trent Park, Go Ape

Founder Ian Puddick asked us to emphasize his distillery's back story for this new edition, and it's certainly unique and sets him apart from the legions of small gin producers in the UK.

Originally he had a plumbing business – and he still does – for which years ago he bought a 150-year-old-old derelict bakery to convert into an office. During the building work, he removed a dangerously unstable chimney, and was sued by a neighbour who claimed to have owned the dangerous chimney. Ian says that during the dispute, his lawyer discovered that the bakery once made illicit gin on the site in Pymmes Mews, London N13. He tracked down the bakery family and their descendants, one of whom was young Barry, seen in the photo above with his dad (Grandad Tom Maysh) on a penny farthing bicycle. For good continuity, Ian also got hold of a penny farthing and had himself photographed recently with his son (see opposite, top left).

He also got hold of the recipe used to make the illicit gin. The original recipe for the illegal gin had only four botanicals, and

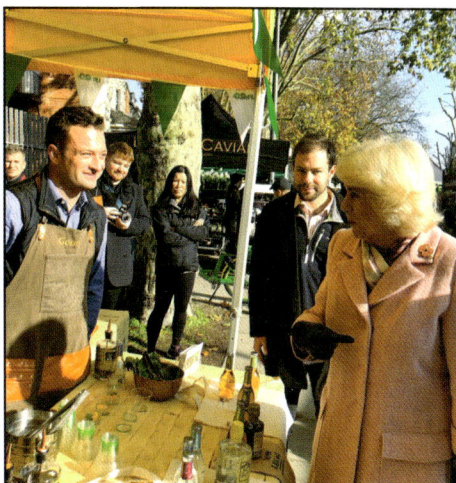

Ian has re-used them faithfully except for one: stinging nettles – a red herring in the old recipe only recently found out.

The gin is still bottled, hand-labelled and wax sealed in the plumbing business office which doubles as a 'bonded warehouse'. Ian and his team also do plumbing work on the side, so this can claim to be the only plumber-distilling business in the country.

He's proud that he supplies his products, which include rum and whisky, to Buckingham Palace, Harrods, the Ministry of Defence, the House of Lords, the Tower of London, Windsor Castle, Fortnum & Mason, The Foreign Office and the British Army. Ian has plenty of celebrity customers too – see the inside front cover of this edition.

Ian's core product, Old Bakery Gin (previous page, left), is a classic, citrus-led London Dry which is great to sip at room temperature as well with a mixer. He recommends serving it with Merchant's Heart Floral Aromatics tonic, a slice of pink grapefruit, fresh basil and plenty of ice – how it's served at Buckingham Palace.

Each year, on the last Saturday of June, they hold the Enfield Gin Festival. It now includes rums from across the UK as well as gins, with only small artisinal brands selling their wares.

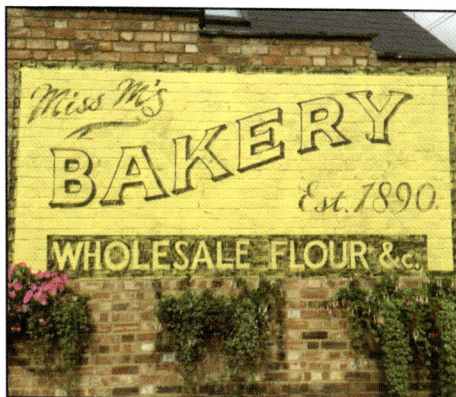

Fort Gin and The Portsmouth Distillery

Portsmouth, Hampshire
Distillery

ESSENTIAL INFORMATION
Key botanicals (Fort Gin): elderflower,
    gorse flower, sea radish
    (Tudor Gin): dandelion, hemp seed,
    hazelnut, cherry
Output: not disclosed
Location: Coastguard Casemate, Fort
    Cumberland, Fort Cumberland Road,
    Southsea, Hants, PO4 9LD
Telephone: 02392 733339
Email: info@theportsmouthdistillery.com
Website: www.theportsmouthdistillery.com
Facebook: www.facebook.com/
    PortsmouthDistillery
Instagram: @portsmouthdistillery
Twitter: @pompeystill

Opening hours:
Tuesday-Saturday 0900-1600

Other reasons to go: Spinnaker Tower,
Hawk Conservancy Trust, The Great Hall

*T*he Portsmouth Distillery is an award-winning rum and gin producer, based in the historic monument that is 18thC Fort Cumberland, surrounded by the sea and representing centuries of naval history. Fort Gin is made with three key botanicals that grow within the Fort itself; Tudor Gin is made using botanicals that would have been on the *Mary Rose* when she sank off Portsmouth in 1545.

Portsmouth's connection with the Royal Navy goes back to the reign of Henry VIII. Given the equally long association between the navy and gin, it is perhaps surprising that only in 2018 did the first modern gin distillery open in the city.

The city is full of historic interest, from Henry VIII's Southsea Castle to The Historic Dockyard, which houses the wreck of the Mary Rose as well as the restored *HMS Warrior* and Admiral Nelson's flagship *HMS Victory*. All are a must to visit in combination with the distillery.

Portsmouth Distillery was started by three friends, two of whom – Vince Noyce and Giles Collighan – are ex-naval officers. The third member of the team, Dick Oatley, has a background in the spirits industry.

The distillery is in the vaulted casements of Fort Cumberland, which is in Eastney at the SE tip of Portsmouth. The pentagonal Georgian fort was built to prevent invasion forces from landing in Langstone Harbour to attack the dockyard overland. The fort is currently owned by English Heritage and a limited number of tours of the distillery are available throughout the year. See the website for details.

Willow Tree Gin and Willow Tree Distilling

Sandy, Bedfordshire
Distillery

ESSENTIAL INFORMATION

Key botanicals (Willow Tree Gin): juniper, coriander, cassia bark, cubeb, lemon peel, lemon thyme, Thai basil, plus five secret ingredients

Output: not disclosed

Location: Trumpetons Farm (Franklins Farm Shop), Thorncote Green, Sandy, SG19 1PU

Telephone: 07826 518601

Email: eloise@willowtreedistilling.co.uk

Website: www.willowtreedistilling.co.uk

Facebook: www.facebook.com/willowtreegin

Instagram: @willowtreegin

Opening hours:

By appointment, or general opening hours
Friday (bookings only)
Saturday 1100-1500
Sunday 1100-1500

Other reasons to go:

Franklins Farm Shop, The Dairy Cafe, The Flower Mill

Willow Tree Distilling was established in 2016 on the family farm in Stanbridge as Bedfordshire's first distillery. They moved premises in 2020, and are now based in the little hamlet of Thorncote Green. Willow Tree Gin is lovingly handcrafted in small batches, using a combination of 12 botanicals including freshly-picked herbs from the family farm. Smoking the botanicals gives the gin its distinctive flavour.

Sustainability is a big part of the Willow Tree ethos. They recycle their cooling water from the distillation process, compost their used botanicals and donate a portion of the sale of every 50-cl bottle towards planting new trees in the Forest of Marston Vale. Willow Tree's recommended perfect serve is: ice, 50 ml Willow Tree Gin, 200 ml Indian tonic, a slice of lemon, and a Makrut lime leaf to garnish.

The distillery also holds tours and gin-making courses. Customers have the chance to choose from more than 60 botanicals and use their own mini still to create their own unique gin. They also offer private hire for corporate events and celebrations, alongside a pop-up bar available for hire on/off site.

Willow Tree Gin can be bought from the distillery itself, their online shop, Bedfordshire Waitrose branches and shops, and bars and restaurants in Bedfordshire (see their website for the full list of stockists).

Pure Sussex Gin and Harley House Distillery

Seaford, East Sussex
Distillery

ESSENTIAL INFORMATION

Key botanicals (Pure Sussex Gin): juniper, coriander, cardamom, cinnamon, cubeb, lemon, grapefruit, ginger, vanilla, honeysuckle flower, ginger, frankincense

Output: 6,000 bottles a year

Location: Sutton Road, Seaford, BN25 4QH

Telephone: 01323 491998

Email: info@harleyhousedistillery.co.uk

Website: www.harleyhousedistillery.co.uk

Facebook: www.facebook.com/harleyhousedistillery

Instagram: @harleyhousedistillery

Twitter: @harleyhousegin

Opening hours:
Visit by appointment only

Harley House is a small-batch artisan distillery based on the south-east coast in Seaford, East Sussex. Started in 2017 by distiller Adam Cowley and co-founder Heidi Cowley, they produce a range of spirits including gin, rum, vodka and liqueurs. The distillery prides itself on creating unique produce that showcases the local area and leaves a lasting memory on the tastebuds. This includes making their own base spirit from scratch for a truly handmade product – fairly rare for a small UK distillery. Water used in production is sourced from an aquifer in the South Downs and used in each batch of gin. Their flagship Pure Sussex Gin has won multiple awards including IWSC Silver Award in both 2019 and 2020, and a 2-Star Great Taste Award in 2020. In 2021 it was also awarded Silver in the London Spirits competition. They also recently won Silver award at the London Spirits Competition 2022 for their Curiosity Series Hedgerow Gin and Prohibition Spiced Rum.

For a classic G&T, Adam and Heidi recommend mixing a measure of Pure Sussex Gin (left, right-hand bottle) with plenty of ice, a few pieces of grapefruit zest and topped up with a premium tonic. It also works well when mixed with apple juice, a dash of lime juice, fresh mint, and some slices of lime to create a Sussex Mojito.

Their signature spirit range includes the Pure Sussex Gin, Sussex Blue Gin (opposite, top left) and Honeysuckle & Hibiscus gin, as well as other seasonal or small batch additions such as Sussex Sloe Gin, Rhubarb & Ginger Gin Liqueur and a Clementine Gin (opposite, middle).

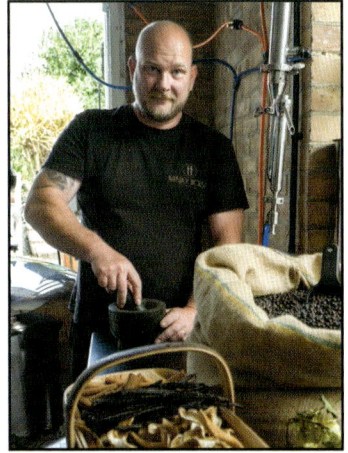

The Curiosity Range (below) showcases Harley House's creative distilling, with various different flavour offerings. These include Indian Spiced Mango, Raspberry & Elderflower, Strawberry, Lemon and Hedgerow Gins, and a Kaffir Lime Vodka.

This range is ever-evolving, and often new batches are made after the public have suggested and voted for their favourite flavours.

All Harley House spirits can be purchased through their online store for delivery nationwide. They also have a range of gift packs, from multiple bottle and glassware boxes to miniature selection packs.

Greensand Ridge Gin and Distillery

Tonbridge, Kent
Distillery

There's much in a name when it comes to Greensand Ridge Gin (next page, bottom), so-called after the hills that surround the Weald of Kent. Will Edge, who grew up in the area, has gone the extra mile to distil a sense of place into his gin by sourcing ingredients from the Weald's orchards, nutteries and hedgerows. Even the bottle design, with its mellow greens and blues, and sunburst gold writing, is inspired by the area's rolling hills.

The name also reflects their sustainable ethos – not just a marketing buzz word in this case but the lifeblood of the brand, feeding into every bit of Will's gin-making process. For the energy-intensive process of distillation they use 100 per cent renewable power; no chemicals are used to clean their stills, and they recycle or reuse almost all their materials; waste fills just one bin bag every eight weeks. Will even works with local farmers to turn their excess crop into brandies and *eau-de-vie.*

In a crowded market, sustainability sets Greensand apart at the moment, but Will is just as concerned with flavour – spending hours at a time in his distillery eking the most out of his botanicals. These include eight local ingredients – bay laurel, poppy seeds, oak moss, hawthorn, berries, cobnuts, rosehips, honey and gorse – reinforced by more traditional botanicals such as juniper, coriander, cardamom and

cassia bark. The result is a well-balanced London Dry Gin with a hint of nuttiness, which Will recommends serving with a bay leaf and a few bruised juniper berries. They also produce seasonal gins.

Inspired by the growing number of entrepreneurial distillers in the gin renaissance, Will – who has a background in IT and finance – finally packed up his corporate job in 2016 to turn his 15-year hobby of making alcohol into a career, first doing a Masters in Brewing and Distilling at Heriott-Watt. The evocative nature of gin made it a natural spirit of choice for Will, although he is also making an *eau de vie* (called Raspberry Ghost, top right) flavoured with Kentish raspberries; brandies from apples and plums; and a golden rum.

This microdistillery is a charming place to visit, sitting just below the Greensand Ridge in the village of Shipbourne, in a former Victorian coaching house – with an enchanting courtyard and sweeping views across the Weald. The Greensand Ridge Gin Experience offers genuine insight into the complexity of the distillation process, introducing guests to the history of gin and the nature of botanicals in the teaching area (previous page, bottom), before enabling them to distil their own gin from the huge range of 40 botanicals.

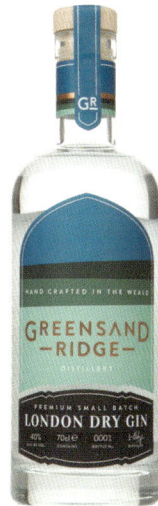

Campfire Gin and
The Puddingstone Distillery

Wilstone, Hertfordshire
Distillery

ESSENTIAL INFORMATION

Key botanicals (Campfire Gin): juniper, coriander, orange peel, grapefruit peel, roasted hazelnut, golden berry, lavender, rooibos

Output: 12,000 bottles a year

Location: Unit 1, Artisan Workshops, Lower Icknield Way, Tring, HP23 4NT

Telephone: 01442 502033

Email: hello@puddingstonedistillery.com

Website: www.puddingstonedistillery.com

Facebook: www.facebook.com/puddingstonedistillery

Instagram: @campfiregin

Twitter: @campfiregin

Opening hours:
Friday-Saturday 0930-1700

Other reasons to go:
Ivinghoe Beacon, Natural History Museum at Tring, College Lake, National Trust (Ashridge Estate)

In November 2016, Ben and Kate Marston opened the doors of Puddingstone Distillery in Tring, Hertfordshire's first gin distillery. Their Campfire Gin range has now amassed more than 30 international spirits awards. In 2019 they won the World's Best Martini Challenge with their London Dry gin and in 2021 were awarded the prestigious title of The Gin Guide's Distillery of the Year.

The couple's decision to establish their own working distillery rather than outsource production was driven by the desire to control all the creative processes, from distilling to brand-building. The brand name, Campfire, was influenced by memorable experiences sipping gin outdoors by open fires. As for the name Puddingstone, this is a rare geological feature found primarily in Hertfordshire and thought to have the ability to ward off evil spirits.

The great outdoors defines the distillery ethos: to create exceptional gins and still be mindful of community and environment. This is reflected in many facets of a business that, from day one, has adopted sustainable practices.

Since 2017, the Puddingstone team has collaborated with local wildlife trusts. Ultrasonic Gin, for example, has a bat conservation theme and uses ultrasound to increase extraction of botanical flavour and aroma, lowering botanical input mass.

Visit the distillery on a Friday or Saturday and you can see Annie, Isabella and Amelia, the three working stills named after great female pioneers – or attend one of their tours or cocktail masterclasses.

The original citrus, juniper-forward Campfire London Dry gin has now been

joined by a smooth, robust Navy Strength (bottom right) and complex Cask Aged gin (middle right). Barrels for the cask-aged gin are sourced directly from Kings County Distillery, selected for the soft vanilla taste they bring to the gin. Rounding up the quartet is an Old Tom gin (below left), the last of the Campfire range to be developed and a re-creation of what Puddingstone Distillery would have made as a rural distillery back in the 17thC.

In late 2021 the distillery moved from its original 50-cl bottle format to a 70-cl bottle – better value.

Each of the gins have been created not only to work in simple tonic-based serves but in more complex cocktails – an approach that shapes botanical selection, ratios, and ABV percentage.

The River Test Distillery

Longparish, Hampshire
Distillery

William Plows writes: River Test Gin, launched in 2019 by Jon and Sarah Nelson (below right), is located on the banks of the River Test. Equipped with ambition and a passion for their part of Hampshire, they decided to create a local distillery that would capture the essence and character of the local environment.

In 2017, they went to Sunderland to do a course on the basics of distilling gin. Fast-forward to 2022, the duo have released three different gins, won numerous awards, been featured in Richard Hammond's *Britain's Beautiful Rivers* television series, and partnered with Craft Gin Club, one of Britain's largest craft gin retailers. Rarely has the term 'fallen into place' been so appropriate.

River Test's original gin, a traditional London Dry (left, and front cover), is composed of eleven individually-selected botanicals, some of which are foraged from the surrounding countryside. Most notable is the meadowsweet flower, found on the banks of the gin-clear River Test, which is infused into the gin. With a floral taste and a hint of honey, the River Test London Dry is smooth and best served over ice with a premium tonic. This gin is widely praised and won England's Best London Dry Gin at the World Gin Awards 2020.

Their London Dry is joined by another show-stopper, Chalkstream Gold Gin (opposite, middle right). Also showcasing local flavours, the gold medal-winning gin is

distilled with Maris Otter Barley, harvested from the fields around the distillery.

River Test's third release, Sunset Citrus Gin (top right) is zestier than the others, combines the citrus flavour of pink grapefruit and pomelo with the gentle sweetness of rosehip. Each gin is bottled in River Test's bespoke, clean-cut bottle specially designed with a unique pattern to boast the crystal-clear nature of the local river. See below, and the guide's front cover.

There have been some bumps along the way, but Jon and Sarah have also enjoyed their fair share of success, and are now planning for growth. New plans for a purpose-built distillery, visitor centre and experience are progressing well.

Twisted Nose Gin and Winchester Distillery

Winchester, Hampshire
Distillery

ESSENTIAL INFORMATION

Key botanicals (Twisted Nose Gin): juniper, coriander seed, liquorice root, cassia bark, grapefruit peel, fennel seed, lavender, watercress

Output: not disclosed

Location: Nickel Close, Winchester, SO23 7RJ

Telephone: 01962 920290

Email: hi@winchesterdistillery.co.uk

Website: www.winchesterdistillery.co.uk

Facebook: www.facebook.com/ WinchesterDistillery

Instagram: @winchester_distillery

Twitter: @WinchDistillery

Opening hours:
Booking required for distillery tours

Other reasons to go: Winchester cathedral and other sights of the historic capital of Wessex

Follow the River Itchen from its source and you will find Winchester Distillery, near the historic cathedral city at the western end of the great chalk swathe of the South Downs National Park.

Ancient bedrock, broad flat downlands and the purest freshwater springs combine to create an extremely rare and special local ecosystem that provides an abundance of the key ingredient in their award-winning Twisted Nose Gin (below): watercress. Growing throughout the region, the Latin name for watercress is *Nasturtium officinale*, derived from 'nasus' meaning nose and 'tortus' meaning twisted, referring to the effect of the peppery taste on the nasal passages. It makes an assertive, fresh G&T, especially if served with Fever-Tree elderflower tonic and a slice of pink grapefruit. Or, when combined with vermouth, it makes a stinger of a Dry Martini.

Paul makes nine other core products in his distillery: Winchester 'Round Table' Dry Gin uses 25 (secret) medieval botanicals, and eight other gins under the Winchester Distillery brand including a classic London Dry, Old Tom, Navy strength 'Gunpowder' gin using gunpowder tea from the local tea merchant, Sloe gin and four limited edition seasonal expressions. Rums, brandies and whiskey are soon to be released. Tours of the distillery can be booked on their website. It includes a talk on the history and process of gin-making, with a tasting session.

Eccentric Gin Distillery

Caerphilly
Distillery

ESSENTIAL INFORMATION
Key botanicals (Madame Geneva): juniper, coriander, lemon peel, orange peel, grapefruit, meadowsweet, sunflower
Output: 4,000-5,000 bottles a year
Location: Unit D, Pontygwindy Industrial Estate, Pontygwindy Road, CF83 3HU
Telephone: 07814 166983
Email: rob@eccentricgin.com
Website: www.eccentricgin.co.uk
Facebook: www.facebook.com/ EccentricGin
Twitter: @EccentricGin

Opening hours:
Monday-Friday 0800-1530
Can collect gin by arrangement on weekends

Other reasons to go: Caerphilly Castle, Llancaiach Fawr, Brecon Mountain Railway

Tom Newman built The Eccentric Gin Distillery in 2014 in the cellar of his pub, The Wheatsheaf Rooms in Llantrisant. His signature gin, Madame Geneva (middle bottle), is a Genever-style gin distilled with water from the Ty-Nant River which runs close to the building. Madame Geneva is made with locally sourced marchalan, Welsh for 'wild sunflower', which gives the gin a subtle sweetness and bitterness. Eccentric Gin's mixologist, Josh, recommends serving a double shot of the gin with a slice of orange and a dash of tonic to taste. For a cocktail, serve the gin in a Martini: add 60 ml of Madame Geneva to 10 ml of dry vermouth, a dash of orange bitters with a lemon twist and sprig of rosemary to garnish.

Eccentric Gin also produce their own Old Tom-style gin (far left bottle), ironically named Young Tom. The spirit is twice distilled with Celt Experience Ogham Willow Beer and then barrel-aged and vapour infused with fennel, wild sunflower root and star anise. It then rests for six weeks to allow the flavours to develop. Limbeck Gin (second from left) is made with blue ginger, citrus, tarragon and Seville orange. The botanicals are rested in old Burgundy French oak casks, which give the gin a smooth texture and a subtle peach colour.

All the gins can be bought from various shops around Wales and the online shop. At £30 is Cardiff Dry Gin (right-hand bottle) which, at its inception, was a new style of gin using fennel as one of its key botanicals, plus rosemary, sorrel, liquorice, lemongrass and verbena – great as an aperitif. The gin was chosen by a cross-section of people from South Wales who carried out multiple tastings to come up with the final flavour.

The Dyfi Distillery

Dyfi, Machynlleth
Distillery

ESSENTIAL INFORMATION
Key botanicals (Dyfi Original Gin): juniper,
  bog-myrtle, pine shoots
Output: 10,000 bottles a year
Location: Corris, Machynlleth, SY20 9RF
Telephone: 01654 761551
Email: danny@dyfidistillery.com
Website: www.dyfidistillery.com
Facebook: www.facebook.com/
  DyfiDistillery
Instagram: @dyfidistillery
Twitter: @DyfiDistillery

Opening hours:
April-October
  Monday-Sunday 1000-1700
For other opening times, check the website

Other reasons to go:
Cader Idris, Southern Snowdonia, ospreys,
kites, dolphins

The wild beauty of Dyfi (pronounced Dovey) Valley would seem more at home in New Zealand than Wales's west coast. As well as being the country's only UNESCO World Biosphere Reserve, it boasts some of the cleanest water, darkest skies and lowest population counts in Europe. So beautiful, in fact, that when Pete Cameron came here over 40 years ago to study biology and botany, he forgot to leave. Meanwhile, his brother Danny (both pictured bottom left) had a career in the world of spirits and wine (earning himself a knighthood from the President of Portugal for his services to Portuguese wine). When they decided to go into business together in 2015, creating award-winning gins with an intense sense of place was a natural step in pooling their resources.

They set out to produce a spirit that reflected the beauty of the area: a Dovey Native Botanical Gin. Mission accomplished as far as we're concerned: a sip of their Pollination Gin (top right) is an almost synaesthetic experience. It's crafted from 29 botanicals, 20 of which are foraged from the valley – with the taste conjuring up freshly-cut herbs and wildflowers. As a G&T it's best served at a ratio of 1:3 with a simple tonic, and in a Martini its nothing short of stunning.

Alongside the Botanical Gin, Dyfi Distillery also produce Hibernation Gin and

a Navigation Gin. Their Hibernation Gin (middle) is botanically derived from their wild fruit harvest, and after distillation is aged in a single 100-year old White Port Cask. At 57% strength, their Navigation Gin tames its wild coastal character by a period of maturation in a 140-year old Madeira barrel. The current line-up is completed by Dyfi Original, whose local pine forest notes nod towards classicism, but give it a character of its own.

All these gins are hand-made using a custom-built still from the Black Forest (all powered by green energy) which allows for an individual and precise approach to each distillate. Every bottle is also signed and numbered by the family to guarantee authenticity.

The distillery is open to visitors every day from April to October without appointment, and some days in winter. While they don't offer formal tours, there is always a warm welcome from the family, as well as the opportunity to taste the range and chat about their highly individual combination of foraging and distillation.

Dà Mhìle Gin and Distillery

Llandysul, Ceredigion
Distillery, shop and tasting room

ESSENTIAL INFORMATION

Key botanicals (Dà Mhìle Botanical Gin):
juniper, coriander, cardamom, citrus,
fennel, sage, star anise, peppermint,
chamomile, dandelion, elderflower,
gorse, rose petal, red clover, white clover

Output: 4,000 bottles a year

Location: Glynhynod Farm, Llandysul,
Ceredigion, SA44 5JY

Telephone: 01239 851998

Email: hi@damhile.co.uk

Website: www.damhile.co.uk

Facebook: www.facebook.com/DaMhile

Instagram: @damhiledistillery

Twitter: @DaMhile

Opening hours:
Monday-Friday 1000-1700
Saturday 0930-1600

Other reasons to go: National Wool
Museum, Skanda Vale, West Wales Museum
of Childhood, Coed Y Foel Woodland Trust

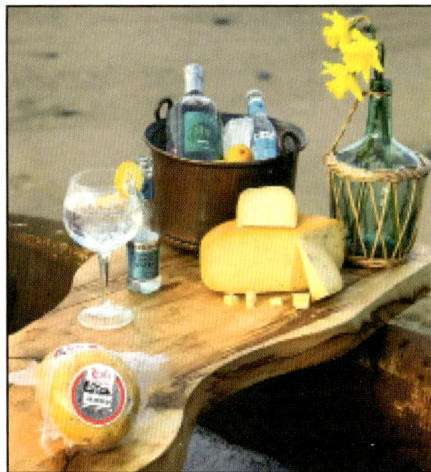

John Savage-Onstwedder came to Wales from Holland in 1981, with an interest in organic farming. He settled at Glynhynod Farm in Ceredigion with a focus on making artisanal cheese using raw milk and local produce. In 1992, he branched out to spirits, commissioning the Springbank Distillery in Campbeltown to produce the world's first organic whisky. In 1999 Dà Mhìle (pronounced da-vee-lay), Gaelic for 2,000, was released to celebrate the new millennium.

John spent the following years focussing on his cheese, until 2006 when he applied for a distiller's licence, one of the first for a 350-litre still in the UK. The distillery was opened in 2012 on John's farm, run by his oldest son, John-James, who trained at Kilchoman Distillery in Scotland, and head distiller Mike Melrose.

Dà Mhìle Botanical Gin was the distillery's second release, after its Orange 33 liqueur, and is distilled in a still powered by a wood-fired steam boiler. The process is slow, taking five to eight hours, but Mike believes it allows as much flavour as possible to be extracted from the botanicals. He recommends serving the gin with a quality tonic and mint.

The second gin was Dà Mhìle Organic Seaweed Gin, launched on St David's Day in 2014. This gin was inspired by a seaweed cheese they had created and is distilled with seaweed hand picked from the Celtic coast. It's then infused with garden herbs for three weeks. The product is triple-filtered before being bottled and emits a light green hue.

Dà Mhìle offers distillery tours which run from Monday to Friday from 12 pm to 3 pm – advanced booking is advised, see the website for details. They also have a shop and tasting room, open Monday to Friday from 10 am to 4 pm, and Saturdays from 9.30 am.

Cygnet Gin, Distillery and Juniper Place

Swansea
Distillery, restaurant and bar

ESSENTIAL INFORMATION

Key botanicals (Cygnet Gin): juniper, coriander seed, liquorice root, cardamom seed, almond, lemon peel, lime peel, orange peel, pink grapefruit peel, chamomile

Output: 10,000+ bottles a year

Location: 1 York Street, Swansea, SA1 3LZ

Telephone: 01792 464111

Email: sales@cygnet-distillery.co.uk

Website: www.cygnet-distillery.co.uk

Facebook: www.facebook.com/ cygnetdistillery

Instagram: @cygnet_distillery

Opening hours:
Monday-Sunday 1000-2200

Other reasons to go: National Waterfront Museum, Swansea Bay (opposite, top right), Mumbles Pier, Oystermouth Castle

Cygnet Gin (below left) was launched in March 2018, but its history goes back as far as the 19thC, when local Swansea men Peter Wakely and William Lee were brought together by their efforts to cure cholera. Wakely knew about the power of spring water and herbs to ward off infection and Lee knew about distilling. Together they worked on infusing their ingredients to create what they hoped would be an effective antidote to the dreaded disease.

Their spirit lives on: Dai Wakely is the descendant of Peter and he created Cygnet Gin with co-founder David Bellis, using a recipe based on his forebear's. Dai, the Master Distiller, was in the hospitality and drinks trade for 15 years, learning mixology along the way. He developed Cygnet Gin alongside Burleighs Gin distiller, Jamie Baxter (page 106), using Welsh spring water. Cygnet claims to be the first microdistillery in South Wales to create, bottle and sell its own gin on the premises.

The distillery offers gin experiences for all budgets. The free Distillery Tour lasts 30 minutes and includes a meet and greet in the Juniper Place restaurant (next page, bottom left) after which you will be taken through to the distillery. Here, you learn about the history of Cygnet, its distilling and bottling process and how it gets to the shelf.

For £37, you can take part in a two-hour Cygnet Masterclass, which starts with the Distillery Tour. You are then escorted back to Juniper Place where you can enjoy a meal from the Light Bites and Bar Menu with a view of the 300-litre still (next page, middle right). This is followed by a guided gin tasting with Dai where you try

three gins and a gin cocktail. You receive a certificate on completion of the masterclass and have the option to buy a bottle of Cygnet Gin with a 10 per cent discount.

To get the full three-hour Cygnet Experience, you pay £55 for a guided tour, a two-course lunch, dinner or afternoon tea in Juniper Place, followed by a gin tasting. You then 'get to know' the botanicals used in Cygnet Gin and learn how to make a perfect serve cocktail from scratch. You then have the option to buy a bottle of Cygnet Gin at a 20 per cent discount.

Welsh Witch Gin and Wild Moon Distillery

Wrexham, North Wales
Distillery

ESSENTIAL INFORMATION

Key botanicals (Welsh Witch Gin): juniper, coriander, lemon, orange, lemon thyme, pink peppercorn, wild gorse, wormwood, Welsh water and moon magic

Output: 2,000 bottles a year

Location: Brymbo, Wrexham, North Wales

Telephone: not disclosed

Email: enquiries@wild-moon.co.uk

Website: www.wild-moon.co.uk

Facebook: www.facebook.com/welshwitchcraftspirits

Instagram: @welshwitch_craftspirits

Opening hours: not open to the public yet

Wild Moon's range of award-winning gins and rum is handcrafted in the Welsh countryside at Wild Moon Distillery. Launched in 2019 by Jade, the Welsh Witch herself, she sets her distillery apart by nurturing a distinct connection with Mother Earth, with a distilling process charged by the moon, natural flavours and a premium taste. Each bottle of Welsh Witch Gin is allowed to mature over a full moon cycle, and is crafted from natural botanicals plus Wales' most precious resource – its pure water. Wild Moon takes inspiration from the Celtic Pagan Wheel of the Year which celebrates the seasons. Each season offers the botanicals to make their drinks.

All bottles are hand corked and waxed by Jade, in a bottle with eye-catching mythical branding. All their gins are priced at £36.00. Pair with a light premium tonic, soda or lemonade.

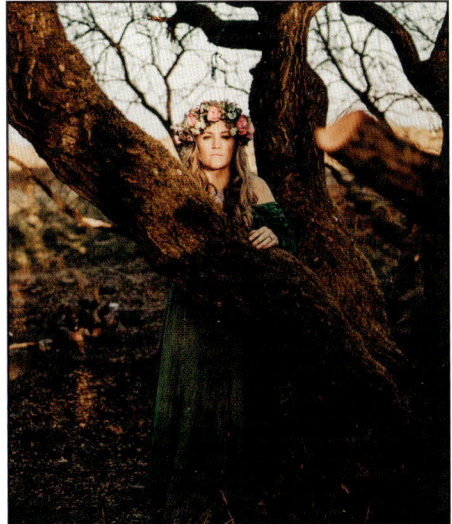

Shining Cliff Gin and White Peak Distillery

Ambergate, Derbyshire
Distillery, shop and tours

ESSENTIAL INFORMATION

Key botanicals (Shining Cliff Original Gin):
juniper, coriander, liquorice, lemon, orange,
elderberry, bilberry, bay, rosehip, lime tree
leaf, linden flower, Derbyshire mayflower

Output: 10,000 bottles a year

Location: Derwent Wire Works, Matlock
Road, Ambergate, DE56 2HE

Telephone: 01773 856918

Email: info@whitepeakdistillery.co.uk

Website: www.whitepeakdistillery.co.uk

Facebook: www.facebook.com/
whitepeakdistillery

Instagram: @whitepeakdistillery

Twitter: @whitepeakwhisky

Opening hours:

Distillery
Monday-Saturday 1100-1700

Tours (booking required)
Thursdays, Fridays and Saturdays

Other reasons to go:
Cromford Canal, The Heights of Abraham

White Peak claims to be the first full-scale craft distillery in the Peak District and takes much inspiration from its Derbyshire surroundings. Local folklore says in the late 17thC, the ancient woodlands of Shining Cliff (from which White Peak's gin takes its name) were home to Luke and Betty Kenny and their eight children. They were charcoal burners who travelled from Nottingham each winter for work and the favourite location for their movable hut was the 2,000-year-old yew tree that features on the Shining Cliff Gin bottle (bottom left). The label also carries the tagline 'Rock-a-Bye Baby', referring to the lullaby Betty sang to her babies as they slept in the boughs of the yew tree while she worked.

The gin is distilled with botanicals which White Peak say are inspired by the Shining Cliff woods, including rosehip, bilberry, elderflower, linden flower, and mayflower. In fact, the botanicals are bought in commercially, with the exception of mayflower, which is foraged once a year. They use the vapour infusion distillation method to capture these delicate flavours. Co-founders Max and Claire recommend sipping the gin neat, or mixing with a premium tonic and garnishing with a slice of fresh orange peel or pink grapefruit.

They also produce three other small batch gins in their Shining Cliff range – Citrus (opposite, top right), Spiced (opposite, bottom right), and Bakewell Pud (opposite, bottom left, left-hand bottle). The latter takes inspiration from the nearby town of Bakewell and incorporates English cherries, almonds and raspberries to imitate the classic Bakewell Pudding. The botanicals give the gin a natural pink hue. As the

flavours are complex in their own right, Max and Claire suggest simply serving with a premium tonic over ice and raspberries.

White Peak also produces limited edition seasonal gins, including a barrel-aged Winter Gin and a Riverside Gin, which is made with local hand-foraged botanicals and supports the Derbyshire Wildlife Trust.

White Peak offers distillery tours and tastings, priced at £15. The tours are largely about whisky production, but they do offer a chance to see the gin still, Betty, and to take part in a guided tasting of the gins. Tours run in groups of up to 16 people and last for approximately one hour to 90 minutes. They're held on Thursdays, Fridays and Saturdays.

The Shining Cliff Gin range is available to buy on their website, or from their Distillery Shop, where they also sell gifts, glassware and other small batch craft spirits.

Bucks Brothers Gin

Buckinghamshire
Craft producer and mobile bar

ESSENTIAL INFORMATION

Key botanicals (Buckinghamshire Dry Gin):
juniper, coriander seed, liquorice root,
cassia bark, lemon peel, orange peel
Output: not disclosed
Location: Little Horwood, Buckinghamshire
Telephone: not disclosed
Email: info@bucksbrothers.co.uk
Website: www.bucksbrothers.co.uk
Facebook: www.facebook.com/
Bucksbrothers
Instagram: @bucksbrothersgin

Opening hours: not open to the public, but
open 24/7 online

Max, Jake and Gus, Buckinghamshire lads born and bred, set up their three-brothers brand in June 2020 as the first lockdown ended, designing their operation to be true to their philosophy – having fun and keeping things simple.

Their signature gin, Buckinghamshire Dry Gin is joined by three gins, two of which are flavoured. Another of their gins is Navy Strength at 58%; the other two are Gin Limone (pleasantly flavoured with lemon) and Pomegranate and Sloe Gin Liqueur, which speaks for itself as their curent best seller.

As we went to press, their pricing ranges between £32 to £36 as standard. Their Navy Strength is fairly priced at £42 due to its higher alcohol percentage, so this is a genuine budget-friendly micro-distiller.

The friendly feel extends to their logo – showing the three brothers depicted as stick men, reflecting their 'have fun, keep things simple' philosophy. The logo adorns their bottles and their pop-up gin bar, continuing the relaxed appeal. Each bottle is hand sealed with wax, then stamped with the logo and given a unique batch and bottle number.

Their pop-up gin bar, fashioned from a horse box, also carries the logo and helps you identify one brother from another. It made a splash at the Blenheim Palace Food Festival in June 2022. You can get your hands on a bottle over at the Bucks Brothers website, or keep an eye out for them at one of the many local Buckinghamshire events they attened. They each have a favourite serve – Jake's for example being quite original: 50 ml Buckinghamshire Dry Gin; 30 ml of honey; 2 sprigs of thyme or rosemary; two sage leaves plus tonic water and ice.

Capreolus Distillery

Cirencester, Gloucestershire
Distillery

ESSENTIAL INFORMATION

Key botanicals (Garden Swift Gin): juniper, grains of paradise, galangal, lime flowers, mullein, rowan berry, home-grown hops, wormwood, fresh organic blood orange zest, plus many more secret ingredients

Output: 13,000 bottles a year

Location: The Mount, Park View, Stratton, Cirencester, GL7 2JG

Telephone: 01285 644477

Email: barney@capreolusdistillery.co.uk

Website: www.capreolusdistillery.co.uk

Facebook: www.facebook.com/CapreolusDistillery

Instagram: @capreolusdistil

Twitter: @CapreolusDistil

Opening hours: not open to the public

The name Capreolus – Latin for roe deer – has become synonymous with fine dining in some of the world's great restaurants and it echoes the quality of this tiny distillery hidden in a Cotswold garden, the work of distiller and owner Barney Wilczak. He shines a light on the terroir (local land) and heritage of his area in exquisite *Eaux de Vie*, wild-fermented fruit brandies that use up to 45 kg of fruit per litre. In keeping with the complexity, integrity and balance of the Eaux de Vie, Barney and his small family team also produce a gin –their acclaimed Garden Swift (next page, middle right). Garden Swift is a cuvee of 34 botanicals brought together in single distillation combining both maceration and vapour extraction. See above left for some of the key players.

With a background in conservation and botany, Barney has brought his experience and meticulous eye to constructing a

rainbow of flavour, based on an idealised set of botanicals in six flavour groups, each creating a whole that is greater than the sum of its parts.

Uncompromising attention to detail characterizes everything made by Capreolus, down to the hand-printed, manually applied letterpress labels.

For something else both typical of the brand and entirely unique, don't miss out on the mulberry wood barrel-aged version of Garden Swift, Hart & Dart.

Brennen and Brown

Cheltenham, Gloucestershire
Distillery and tasting room

ESSENTIAL INFORMATION

Key botanicals (Gin with a Hint of Ginger):
   juniper, ginger, orange and lemon peel
Output: not disclosed
Location: Brennen and Brown Ltd., Unit 2C,
   The Bramery, Alstone Lane, GL51 8HE
Telephone: 01242 370400
Email: info@brennenandbrown.co.uk
Website: www.brennenandbrown.com
Facebook: www.facebook.com/
   brennenandbrowm
Instagram: @brennenandbrown
Twitter: @brennenandbrown

Opening hours:
Tuesday-Thursday 0900-1600
Friday 0900-1900
Saturday 1200-1900

Other reasons to go: Gloustershire,
Warwickshire Steam Railway, Montpellier
District

Ginger is the name of the game here: it's the key botanical in the distillery's flagship gin and so far no other distillery we have come across uses the marvellous root to the same extent. Apart from its wonderful taste, it has a list of health benefits from the scientifically credible, to the possible, to old wives' tales. In the first category is oral hygeine and gut health; in the second are easing muscle aches and arthritis, and possibly lowering blood sugar; in the third are claims that it combats diseases including avian flu.

Distiller Rich Bamber's first venture was in IT: an iPad-based point of sales system. In 2021, while installing an iPad till in a distillery, he asked the distiller if he knew of anyone using ginger to flavour gin. The answer: 'only a hundred years back'. Rich was quickly aboard the craft gin movement, using a pretty miniature copper still, Una, to create small batches of his launch product, Gin with a Hint of Ginger (left). A mouthful starts with juniper, then citrus, and finishes with the warmth of the ginger. Local bars and restaurants started buying, output grew, the range diversified and Una was replaced with rotary evaporator stills, whose gentle action Rich thinks ideal for his particular botanicals.

Brennen and Brown (Rich's grandmothers' maiden names) are savvy marketeers who see separate opportunities in gin tasting and gin making. You can visit their tasting room to sharpen your taste buds against a range of gins, or you can do a gin course ('lab experience'), learning to make your own bespoke gin. They have a well-presented shop, which can be found via their website.

Pinnock Distillery and Castle Gin School

Edgehill, Warwickshire
Distillery and gin school

ESSENTIAL INFORMATION
Key botanicals (Pinnock Dry Gin): juniper, coriander, cardamom seeds, cassia, fennel seeds, cubeb, Seville orange peel, quince, lavender and honey
Output: 2,000-3,000 bottles a year
Location: Edgehill near Kineton, Warwickshire
Telephone: 01295 670255
Email: info@pinnockdistillery.com
Website: www.pinnockdistillery.com
Facebook: www.facebook.com/pinnockgin
Instagram: @pinnockgin
Twitter: @PinnockGin

Opening hours:
Friday 1500-2000
Saturday 1300-1800

Other reasons to go: Edgehill Battlefield, Upton House, Compton Verney, North Cotswolds, Stratford-upon-Avon, Warwick, Royal Leamington Spa

Set in the beautiful Warwickshire countryside, Pinnock Gin is named after the cottage where the small-batch, copper-distilled gin was launched in 2018. A humble beginning – but soon the distillery was winning awards. It has now relocated to Radway Tower at the Castle at Edgehill, which overlooks the infamous civil war battlefield, and is an idyllic Grade II listed structure with views of four counties.

The new venue is perfect for this distillery. Distiller Daniel Beckett was inspired by a 'strong water' recipe book commissioned by Charles I, who fought Parliament at Edgehill. The botanicals in the original Pinnock Dry Gin were inspired by these recipes, and several are genuinely local: lavender sourced from Snowshill, honey from Kineton and quince from Warwick. These botanicals are used with others (see list, left) to create the smooth, complex signature Pinnock Dry Gin (left). Pinnock's other gins are also strongly rooted in the locality and include the multi award-winning Rhubarb and Strawberry, Sloe, Damson and Honey blends. Locals who help source the fruit and berries are rewarded with free bottles.

Using a traditional 40-litre copper alembic still, a small but effective team bottles, labels and wax seals by hand. The distillery's latest enterprise (in partnership with Freespirit Pubs) is the Castle Gin School launched early in 2022. Visitors can hear a talk by the master distiller and enjoy a tasting session, or they can make their own gin under tuition, all at the top of the tower, plus impressive views. The Castle also has rooms where you can stay the night, and a great bar, restaurant and gardens.

Try drinking Pinnock Dry Gin with an orange or a grapefruit garnish. It's also great in a Martini and a Negroni. Pinnock Rhubarb and Strawberry Gin works well when garnished with fresh strawberries. Pinnock Sloe, Damson and Honey Gin (top right) is delicious with lemon in a longer drink, with a lemon tonic for a summery punch, or neat over ice; or even try as a winter hot toddy.

Wardington's Original Ludlow Dry Gin

Ludlow, Shropshire
Distillery

ESSENTIAL INFORMATION
Key botanicals (Wardingtons Original Ludlow Dry Gin): juniper, coriander, cardamom, lemon peel, orange peel, gorse
Output: 55,000 bottles a year
Location: Ludlow, Shropshire
Telephone: 07952 580567
Email: office@ludlowgin.co.uk
Website: www.wardingtons.co.uk
Facebook: www.facebook.com/ wardingtonsoriginal
Instagram: @ludlowdrygin
Twitter: @ludlowdrygin

Opening hours:
Not currently open to the public

This producer's story began with the birth of Wardington's Original Ludlow Gin in the Welsh Marches. From the outset, Wardington's wanted to create premium hand-crafted gins that you could drink neat and savour. They distill gin just as it has been crafted for hundreds of years, using the finest natural botanicals and no artificial colours or flavours. They use traditional copper-pot distillation, and simply add water to bring the gin to bottling strength.

Master distiller and founder, Shaun Ward, knew from the outset that he wanted to create a timeless classic for customers to cherish. He believes that distilling a premium gin is a form of alchemy. He likes his gin straight from the freezer neat in a Martini, or in an ice-laden G&T. Distilling his own juniper-led, no-fuss gin was his priority.

They've created a range of styles, all London Dry, and all made exclusively from natural botanicals distilled with the finest grain spirit. Their classic 'house gin', Ludlow Dry, is perfect as a G&T or as a base for a martini, and is also available in Navy Strength at 57%. Their Elderflower, Chamomile and Lemon Verbena Gin (opposite, middle left) is fresh and floral, and their Earl Grey Gin (opposite, middle right) was released for the Queen's Platinum Jubilee with botanicals harvested from the Scottish highlands, including Bog Myrtle.

Wardington's recently added a premium whisky, vodka and rum to their range (left), all handcrafted and excellent.

From spring 2023, you will be able to book distillery tours and a gin school experience in their new distillery near Ludlow. The move means that they can claim to be the largest craft distillery in the region.

Tranquil Still

Market Drayton, Shropshire
Distillery

ESSENTIAL INFORMATION
Key botanicals (Round the Garden Gin):
  juniper, coriander seed, honeysuckle,
  hibiscus, jasmine, marigold, chilli,
  tangerine zest, lemon, lime
Output: 50 bottles per production week
Location: Market Drayton, North Shropshire
Telephone: 07801 570397
Email: tony@tranquilstill.co.uk
Website: www.tranquilstill.co.uk
Facebook: www.facebook.com/TranquilStill
Instagram: @tranquil_still
Twitter: @Tranquil_Still

Opening hours: not open to the public

In a peaceful setting surrounded by farmland, a short walk from the Shropshire Union Canal, is the wooden shed belonging to the Tranquil Still distillery.

It is one of the few craft distilleries in this guide that controls quality and flavour all the way from grain to glass, producing their own base spirit from a handcrafted grain brew for the very small batches of its gin, vodka and rum. Tony got great feedback on the quality and smoothness of the drinks from early tastings, leading him to seek industry professionals' reactions via blind tastings and entering two of his spirits into the 2022 World Drinks Awards. He was astonished and delighted that both drinks won medals. Chair of Judges David T. Smith noticed the distinctive taste of the base spirit, and when sampling the vodka described it as exceptional and unique.

So, why 'Tranquil Still'? Tony worked as a consultant clinical psychologist specialising in major trauma and later studied for a PhD in family law at Keele, before becoming a full-time single parent. Looking for a new focus, Tony realized that he enjoyed cooking, and that distilling uses similar skills, combining alcohol with different flavours. Distilling became a happy and peaceful enjoyment.

The botanicals chosen for Tony's lead gin, Round the Garden (left), come from memories of his parents' garden, particularly of honeysuckle and hibiscus. Its name emerged when Pete, one of Tony's tasters, likened the medley of botanicals in the gin to walking round their garden.

With proximity to Bradley Farm's 52,000 blueberry bushes plus Shropshire's fame for damson trees – the distillery's

logo features a wind-blasted damson tree (below) – it seemed obvious to create a blueberry gin, (above, third from right) and a damson gin (above, third from left). Both are unsweetened to highlight the fruits' flavours, and some blueberries are even included in the blueberry gin bottles.

A truly exceptional vodka (above, second from left) and a navy-strength, lightly spiced white rum (above, second from right) complete the current Tranquil Still range, although two new gins are in production.

The distillery also makes their 'Tipple Time' gin range, Seaside Rock (above, left) and Bubblegum (above, right). The red, white and blue gins were produced for an RAF summer ball. Tony says, "These two gins are trapdoors which plunge you back into childhood memories, without the sand ruining your stick of rock or bubblegum getting stuck in your hair."

Union Distillers Ltd.
Two Birds Gin, KEEPR's and Dodd's

Market Harborough, Leicestershire
Distillery

ESSENTIAL INFORMATION

Key botanicals (Two Birds London Dry
Gin): juniper, coriander, citrus, plus one
secret ingredient

Output: 1 million bottles a year

Location: E7 Welland Business Park, Valley
Way, Market Harborough, LE16 7PS

Telephone: 01858 463758

Email: sales@twobirdsspirits.co.uk

Website: www.twobirdsspirits.co.uk
www.keeprs.co.uk

Facebook: www.facebook.com/
twobirdsspirits
www.facebook.com/keeprsspirits
www.facebook.com/doddsgin

Instagram: @twobirdsspirits
@keeprsspirits
@doddsgin

Opening hours:
Monday-Friday 0900-1700

Other reasons to go: Harborough Museum,
St Mary in Arden Church, Kelmarsh Hall

David Smith writes: Union Distillers is in the Leicestershire town of Market Harborough, which was also home to a 17thC grammar school and was the staging place for royalist troops before the decisive Battle of Naseby during the English Civil War.

The modern-day distillery was founded by Mark Gamble and Lyn Taylor. Mark's first career was working in a business that designed and fabricated equipment for the food service industry – experience which he found useful when creating his first still, Gerard, which continues to be used every day.

Union Distillers released their first product in 2013, a classic London Dry gin called Two Birds Gin (below, left-hand bottle) and has evolved to include flavoured gins and vodkas such as the popular Watermelon Gin (below, right-hand bottle) and the exotic Passion Fruit Vodka, as well as a spiced rum and an espresso liqueur.

In 2021 it merged with the British Honey Company Plc, known for its award-winning honey-infused spirits range, KEEPR's, and the owners of Dodd's Organic Gins. All of these brands are now produced from Union's distillery alongside several white label spirits for business customers, including some major supermarkets. The company also has a partnership agreement with English Heritage to produce its gins and an affordable luxury spirits portfolio, called 1606.

Burleighs Gin

Nanpantan, Leicestershire
Distillery, bar, shop and gin school

ESSENTIAL INFORMATION
Key botanicals (Burleighs Gin): juniper,
coriander seed, cardamom, orange peel,
burdock root, silver birch
Output: 110,000 bottles a year
Location: The Collection Yard, Bawdon
Lodge Farm, Charley Road, Nanpantan,
LE12 9YE
Telephone: 01530 245402
Email: enquiries@45w.co.uk
Website: www.burleighsgin.com
Facebook: www.facebook.com/burleighsgin
Instagram: @burleighsgin
Twitter: @burleighsgin

Opening hours:
Sunday-Thursday 1030-2330
Friday-Saturday 1030-0130

Other reasons to go: Great Central Railway,
Beacon Hill Country Park, Charnwood
Museum, Manor Farm Park and Woodlands

This distillery produces authentic, premium quality gin, and handcrafts and distills every bottle using traditional techniques.

Its signature recipe is based on botanicals found in the ancient woodland surrounding the distillery, and used in the distillation of the first bottle of Burleighs Gin back in June 2014.

Other offerings in its core range include the Distiller's Cut – which uses the authentic Burleighs botanical recipe to showcase the distiller's craft – and the Burleighs Pink Edition Gin (opposite, bottom) – a floral and delicate creation, inspired by a visit to Tokyo during Hanami, with Japanese cherry blossom, hibiscus, rose and pink grapefruit to the fore.

Burleighs tenacity and creativity has delivered notable success during the last eight years. It has doubled in size, launched over 20 new products and has worked with significant Leicester-based businesses and brands such as Leicester Tigers (opposite, top right) and Leicester City Football Club. The distillery has produced bespoke gins for both sports clubs, as well as a King Richard III Gin inspired by the 15thC monarch discovered in a car park in the city of Leicester.

Burleighs values the community in which it operates and aims to support local organizations and initiatives whenever possible – one of its latest products being an example. The distillery made an exclusive new gin to provide vital funds for the National Forest – one of the boldest environmentally-led regeneration projects in the country. A donation from every bottle goes to the National Forest to support its vision for growing a better,

greener future. Working in partnership with expert foresters, Burleighs developed the botanical mix using its signature recipe as a base, adding in extra ingredients including blackberries, wild cherry and elderflower from nearby forests to create the new offering.

Burleighs has since diversified with the introduction of ready-to-drink cans and new products including a Mulled Christmas Gin, and a Raspberry Edition Gin – produced by steeping the signature gin recipe in raspberries and peaches. Its latest launch is The Mad Hatter's Gin – a bespoke creation to celebrate Age UK Leicester Shire & Rutland's 70th anniversary, supporting thousands of local projects and communities.

They also runs distillery tours and gin tasting sessions, as well as a distilling experience at its gin academy. Guests can create their own unique gin using botanicals of their choice and sample Burleigh's gin and tonics – all with the expert guidance of Burleighs' head distiller.

Redsmith Gin and Distillery

Nottingham, Nottinghamshire
Distillery

ESSENTIAL INFORMATION
**Key botanicals (Redsmith London Dry
    Gin): juniper, coriander, orange, plus six
    secret ingredients**
Output: not disclosed
**Location: Unit 33 Avenue C, Nottingham,
    NG1 1DW**
Telephone: 01158 712545
Email: office@redsmithdistillery.com
Website: www.redsmithdistillery.com/
**Facebook: www.facebook.com/
    RedSmith-Distillery**
Instagram: @redsmithgin
Twitter: @RedSmithDistill

Opening hours:
Visits by appointment only

**Other reasons to go: Nottingham Castle,
Wollaton Hall, City of Caves**

David Smith writes: Redsmith Distillery is in the bustling Creative Quarter of Hockley in the City of Nottingham. This area is also known as The Soho of Nottingham and is home to various fashion and record shops, as well as trendy bars and restaurants.

The distillery was founded in 2015 by Wayne Asher and started life in the small village of Ruddington, before moving to Nottingham in early 2017. Wayne had previously studied engineering, worked in the aerospace industry, and set up a plumbing and heating business. The name Redsmith is a nod to Wayne's metalworking past – and comes from the name for someone who works with copper, as opposed to a blacksmith, who works with iron or steel.

This experience also gave him the skills to build his own first still, Jenny (opposite, top right). Jenny was custom-built and designed over a period of 12 months and includes a ten-plate rectifying column, as well as a carterhead to allow the vapour distillation of botanicals. Wayne also created a smaller still, named Tiny Tess, to assist with product research and development.

Redsmith's London Dry (opposite, bottom) and Nottingham Dry Apple Gin are the distillery's principal gins. The distillery also produces limited releases that fall on the traditional side of the gin spectrum. The latest two are the Redsmith Orange and White Tea Gin (left) and their Licorice Old Tom (opposite, top left). Both gins are based on the London Dry recipe with a twist.

To make Redsmith Orange and White Tea Gin, organic orange zest and white tea added are added as botanicals to the

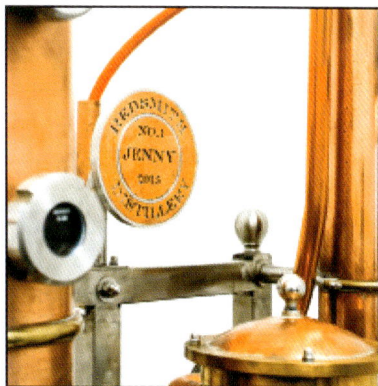

still. Post-distillation, the gin rests with more orange zest before bottling. The resulting gin has a delicate orange hue, and is dry, bright and elegant in taste. The prominent citrus pairs well with the juniper and the white tea delivers a dry, crisp finish.

The Licorice Old Tom Gin is a Redsmith take on what gin may have been like in the times before the London Dry styles became popular. This gin is also based on a tried-and-tested Redsmith recipe and is sweetened with just enough fruit sugar to complement the alcohol, and is rested with licorice root after distillation. The gin acquires a golden yellow colour and has a complex, warm, sweet and woody flavour. You can still taste the juniper, but this gin behaves more like a barrel-aged spirit. It makes a sensational Tom Old Fashioned, and can be enjoyed without a mixer.

The distillery works closely with a local pub to offer gin tastings and educational sessions, as well as tours of the distillery (by appointment only).

Ruddy Fine Gin

Ruddington, Nottingham
Distillery

ESSENTIAL INFORMATION

Key botanicals (Ruddy Fine Lockdown Gin): crab apple, bramley apple, lavender, bay leaf, nettle leaves, raspberry leaves
Output: 8,500 bottles a year
Location: 39 Nottingham South & Wilford Industrial Estate, Ruddington Lane, NG11 7EP
Telephone: 07540 096234
Email: info@ruddyfine.co.uk
Website: www.ruddyfine.co.uk
Facebook: www.facebook.com/RuddyFineGin
Instagram: @ruddyfine
Twitter: @ruddyfinegin

Opening hours:
Monday-Friday 0930-1630
Gin tastings at weekends by appointment only

Other reasons to go: Nottingham Castle, Sherwood Forest, National Watersports Centre, Framework Knitters Museum

When Cheryl and Rory met and sat chatting over gin cocktails while on their first date, they had no idea where their mutual appreciation of gin would take them a few years later. Ruddy Fine Gin came about from a fascination with the flavours and methods involved in creating the spirit, and a desire to make something they could pass on to their children.

Experimenting with a few locally-sourced botanicals soon progressed to a five-litre copper still in their kitchen, and they now develop their range of gins close to home with the help of their still, Marion. Based in the small village of Ruddington in the Nottinghamshire countryside, the Ruddy Fine Distillery is the essence of a small artisan producer. All their gin flavours are still meticulously developed in their own kitchen before being taken down the road to the distillery to be cooked up in batches of just 350 bottles at a time.

Join them at their award-winning distillery for a relaxed evening of gin sampling in their intimate Art Deco style tasting lounge, where you'll learn the story of the Ruddy Fine Distillery, the history of the brand, and taste their gin's unique flavours, served in the most tantilising combinations. These tasting evenings will maximise gin lovers' appreciation of different botanicals and sharpen their sense of taste. Dates are released monthly and can be booked online, with a minimum of six people and maximum of eight.

Ruddy Fine have received a number of awards in 2022: an International Gin Guide Award and three Great Taste Awards. Their Lockdown Gin (left) was shortlisted in the Grocer Magazine for Best New Alcohol Product of 2021. Ruddy Fine has now

become the first guest gin to be available in the Houses of Parliament.

Ruddy Fine Distillery is a family affair, and typical of this is their Ruddy Fine Gin Club and the Ruddy Fine Gin Secret Swillers group. Cheryl and Rory's friends and neighbours sit in their garden reviewing their shortlisted batches to develop the flavours. Their children help build the gift boxes and tidy up the distillery after a long day. The club aims to create an audience of people who appreciate not just gin, but also support Cheryl and Rory's building of their own artisan company.

As a perk, they will be sending out complimentary 20-cl bottles of all their new flavours to members of the Ruddy Fine Gin Club, with feedback requested. A lucky few will be randomly selected during the development phase of new flavours and sent samples of shortlisted batches for their thoughts.

Stratford Gin and Shakespeare Distillery

Stratford-upon-Avon, Warwickshire
Distillery and experiences

ESSENTIAL INFORMATION

Key botanicals (Stratford Gin): juniper, coriander seed, lemon peel, orange peel, rosemary, lovage seed, lemon balm leaf, rose

Output: not disclosed

Location: Unit A, Drayton Manor Drive, Stratford-upon-Avon, CV37 9RQ

Telephone: 01789 336559

Email: tours@shakespearedistillery.com

Website: www.shakespearedistillery.com

Facebook: www.facebook.com/ shakespearedistillery

Instagram: @shakespearedistillery

Twitter: @shakespearedistillery

Opening hours:

Wednesday-Saturday 1000-1700

Sunday 1000-1600

Advanced booking advised for experiences

Other reasons to go: Shakespeare's birthplace, Anne Hathaway's cottage, Church of the Holy Trinity Stratford Butterfly Farm

A distillery in Stratford-upon-Avon calls, of course, for Shakespeare in its name, and Simon Picken also pays homage to The Bard by using botanicals in Stratford Gin (below) that were well known in Tudor England. For example, lovage, known at the time as 'love ache', was used in love potions and as a deodorant, while lemon balm was used for dressing wounds. Tudor England was an interesting time in gin history: at first, distilling was confined to the monasteries and the product was used mainly for medicinal purposes. After the Dissolution of the Monasteries, distilling became a nationwide industry and all social classes started to drink spirits.

The distillery is on the Drayton Manor Farm Estate on the outskirts of Stratford-upon-Avon. They use the single shot method (see page 28). The environmentally-friendly still, Portia (named after *The Merchant of Venice*'s heroine), has a 250-litre capacity and combines heavy insulation to preserve energy with a computer-controlled cooling condenser that lets in just enough water to cool down the vapour. As in many stills, copper is placed in the vapour path so every drop of alcohol comes into contact with it before leaving the still, creating a clean, smooth spirit. At the new distillery, Portia has been joined by her 500-litre big sister, Ophelia (named after the protagonist's love interest in *Hamlet*). The Shakespeare Distillery website sells their full range of gin and rum, along with limited edition distillery specials and gift set options.

Stratford Dry is a herbal gin inspired by the Tudor knot garden. For the perfect G&T, add 50 ml to 100 ml of tonic water, serve over ice, add a wedge of lemon and a

sprig of rosemary. Mulberry Gin Liqueur is inspired by the trees in Shakespeare's Stratford home, and is made by steeping black mulberries in Stratford Dry for several months. Their punchy Rhubarb Gin is tart and delicious: add to lime and ginger ale for a fresh, fruity summer thirst-quencher. The Elderflower & Quince Gin uses quintessentially British flavours and is a great accompaniment to a cheese board, pairing well with aromatic or elderflower tonic and a slice of orange. The distillery also launched Jester, their new British-made rum last year (top, right two bottles), with the range including Jester White Rum, Jester Spiced Rum and Jester Chocolate Rum. A series of barrel-aged rums was to be launched in 2022.

Distillery tours run throughout the week from Wednesday to Sunday and Gin Schools run every weekend, as well as a summer Gin Tasting Cruise and monthly Cocktail Masterclasses.

Judith's at No.1 High Street is their new visitor location in Stratford-upon-Avon town centre, and is the former home of William Shakespeare's daughter Judith. The historical building is now home to their shop and newly-launched Rum School and Gin Tasting experiences.

Tiger Gin

West Midlands

ESSENTIAL INFORMATION
Key botanicals (Tiger Gin): juniper, coriander seed, liquorice root, cassia bark, cinnamon bark, lemon peel, orange peel, nutmeg, plus two secret ingredients
Output: not disclosed
Location: West Midlands
Telephone: 01952 384375
Email: sales@tigergin.co.uk
Website: www.tigergin.com
Facebook: www.facebook.com/tigergin.uk
Instagram: @thetigergin
Twitter: @TheTigerGin

Opening hours: not open to the public

This gin was launched in 2016 after a rocky start – the producers of Tiger Beer challenged the trademark, but distiller JJ Lawrence came out victorious after a long court case. They are now one of the most-followed gin brands on social media.

JJ wanted his gin to be sweet and smooth enough to sip on its own. To achieve this, he uses a higher-than-usual amount of liquorice root, along with seasonal botanicals from around the world which are steeped in neutral grain spirit overnight. The product is then distilled for nine hours to produce an 80% strength gin before it's cut with water to 40%. Try it in a G&T with a slice of orange, or in a Martini.

Tiger Gin also produce Ruby Gin, a pink gin made with British rhubarb. It is best served over ice with rose lemonade or ginger ale.

The gins can be bought from Tiger Gin's website and from wine shops around the country, as well as the Master of Malt website (www.masterofmalt.com).

Cambridge Distillery

Cambridgeshire
Distillery, shop and tailor-made gins

ESSENTIAL INFORMATION

Key botanicals (Cambridge Dry Gin – bottom): juniper, lemon verbena, basil, rosemary, blackcurrant leaf, rose petal

Output: not disclosed

Location: 20-22 High Street, Grantchester, CB3 9NF

Telephone: 01223 751146

Email: info@cambridgedistillery.co.uk

Website: www.cambridgedistillery.co.uk

Facebook: www.facebook.com/ CambridgeDistillery

Instagram: @cambridgegin

Twitter: @CambridgeGin

Opening hours:

The Showroom

Monday-Saturday 1000-1800

Tuesday 1100-1800

Sunday 1000-1600

Other reasons to go: River Cam, Trumpington Meadows, Shepreth Wildlife Park, Wandlebury Country Park

This is a polished operation that claims to be 'the world's first gin tailors'. By this, founders William and Lucy Lowe mean that the distillery enables you (for £400) to create your own 'bespoke' blend. You get a two-hour consultation with William, master distiller, and blind tastings to define your palate. This forms the basis for your gin. After making the first bottle (or bottles), the recipe is then filed so that you can order more.

The distillery uses fresh botanicals from the countryside outside Cambridge – where possible. Each botanical is distilled individually by the partial vacuum method, in less than two-litre batches, to preserve the freshest possible flavour.

They also produce a Seasonal Gin, costing £90 a bottle, which is only made twice a year. The Vintage Spring Summer 2021 edition (opposite, middle) featured lemon balm, hawthron blossom and nettle leaf. Other gins include Japanese Gin (next page, bottom right), combining juniper with traditional Japanese botanicals such as yuzu peel, shiso leaf, sansho pepper and sesame seed.

William Lowe has 20 years' experience in the drinks industry, and managing director Lucy has a marketing and events background. Despite the distillery's international reputation, every bottle is still produced by hand, so it can claim to be a small batch distiller. Curator's Gin, their collaboration with Cambridge University Botanic Garden, was originally only available as an experimental batch of just 600 bottles, but as we went to press is now available online as a permanent fixture of the collection. The botanicals were picked from the university's Botanic Garden and

include lavender, green ginger rosemary, Newton's apple, and lemon balm. A visit to Cambridge itself (which has produced more Nobel prizewinners than France, especially for scientific achievements) combined with a visit to the nearby village of Grantchester, makes an interesting day out. The distillery is in Grantchester, and offers masterclasses, tastings, and a shop. You can also visit their Gin Laboratory (top left and below) at 10 Green Street, Cambridge – see page 211.

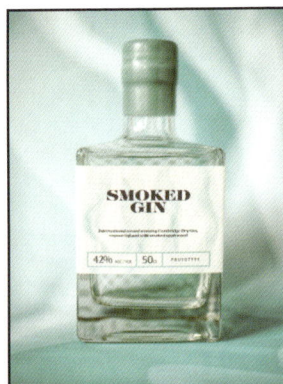

Archangel Gin and Distillery

Fakenham, Norfolk
Distillery

ESSENTIAL INFORMATION

Key botanicals (Archangel Gin): juniper, cardamom, cinnamon, grains of paradise, orange peel, cloves, ginger, verbena, sea buckthorn, plus three secret ingredients
Output: 12,000 bottles a year
Location: The Distillery, Dunton Hall, Fakenham, Norfolk, NR21 7PG
Telephone: 01328 744436
Email: distiller@archangel-distilleries.co.uk
Website: www.archangel-distilleries.co.uk
Facebook: www.facebook.com/ArchangelDistilleries
Instagram: @archangeldistilleries

Opening hours:
Monday-Sunday 0900-1700
Phone to confirm
Distillery tours bookable via the website

Other reasons to go: Norfolk Coast, Pensthorpe Natural Park, Langham Glass merchant, Thursford

Archangel's co-founders, Peter Allingham and Jude De Souza, met in 1994 at ITV in London where Peter was an IT consultant and Jude worked as a statistician. A mutual friend Craig Penn, who runs the Wrecking Coast Distillery, inspired them with the success of his venture and suggested they work together. Their first move was to travel to Holland to learn about distilling. They then converted some disused stables on Peter's family farm into a distillery.

Archangel lies on the last section of the old pilgrimage route to Walsingham Abbey from Castle Acre Priory. Peter and Jude are Roman Catholics, conscious of the monastic tradition of making beers and spirits, so the religious brand name came naturally. There are angels on the labels, and a 19thC Dutch crucifix hangs on the wall of the bottling room.

Peter and Jude use a genever-style recipe to reflect the Dutch influence in Norfolk during the 16th to 19thC. They use local verbena and juniper picked from bushes planted by Peter 20 years ago (next page, middle). In 2016, they planted another 200 juniper bushes, plus 50 sea buckthorn. In 2019, 2,500 blackthorn bushes were planted for sloes. The grain spirit and botanicals are distilled using the single-shot method, after which pure Walsingham water is used to cut the spirit down to 45%.

The first batch of Archangel Gin (left) was made in February 2017. Now, five years later, they have an established following and distribution throughout Norfolk.

To enjoy Archangel at its best, mix 50 ml of the gin with a couple of orange slices, 150 ml of Fever-Tree tonic and plenty

of ice. Archangel also works well as a cocktail base: add 50 ml of the gin to 25 ml of Campari, 75 ml of fresh orange and lemon juice, 2 tbsp of Peruvian marmalade (or Seville will do) and a dash of Angostura orange bitters to make a Paddington Bear (right).

They also produce a limited edition Rhubarb Gin Liqueur (bottom right), made with Norfolk rhubarb steeped in their own vodka for at least four weeks. The product is then blended with Archangel Gin before being filtered twice. This is best served neat, or with ginger ale or Prosecco to make a Rhubarb Royale. Their special winter release, Sloe and Mulberry Liqueur, is made with local fruit and is great as a sipping gin or when added to Prosecco. New lines include an award-winning Plum Gin Liqueur and the Cardinalis, a delicious sloe port.

The gins can be bought from the online shop and can also be found in various shops, bars and restaurants around East Anglia (top) with outlets in London too – see their website for details.

Roundwood Gin and Distillery

Huntingdon, Cambridgeshire
Distillery

ESSENTIAL INFORMATION

Key botanicals (Roundwood Gin): juniper, coriander seed, orange peel, bitter orange peel, elderberry, elderflower

Output: not disclosed

Location: Unit 1, Wennington Lodge Farm, PE28 2LP

Telephone: 01487 829149

Email: info@roundwooddistillery.co.uk

Website: www.roundwooddistillery.co.uk

Facebook: www.facebook.com/ roundwoodgin

Instagram: @roundwoodgin

Twitter: @roundwoodgin

Opening hours: not open to the public

Emily Robertson (next page, bottom right) had been a software developer for several years and was looking for a drastic life change to get her away from commuting and desk work. She shared a love of gin with her partner and co-founder, Rupert (next page, bottom left), and they wanted to make a product that represented rural Cambridgeshire. The result? Roundwood Gin (right), launched in May 2018.

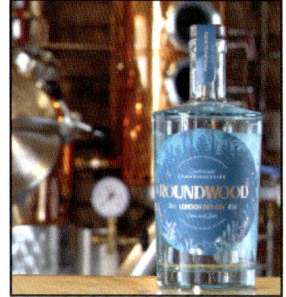

The couple moved to Huntingdon in 2014 for Rupert's job as a manager on the De Ramsey Estate, where they now live, outside of Abbots Ripton, on one side of Wennington Wood, a 180-acre woodland area which they say formed the inspiration for their brand. The woodland has no footpaths, so you have to walk round it, hence Roundwood. They rented a crumbly brick building on the other side of the wood to house the distillery.

While the product was launched in 2018, the process of turning the building into a distillery and perfecting the recipe took 18 months. Emily collated every botanical she'd come across, distilling each individually to find the flavours she enjoyed most. She wanted to create a London Dry that incorporated botanicals inspired by the Wennington woodland and she found that elderberries lifted the dryness of the juniper, providing a sweetness to the gin, while elderflower gave a subtle floral finish.

Emily uses a combination of the maceration and vapour infusion methods (page 28) to ensure the subtle flavours of each botanical are extracted during distillation. The unique copper still has a rectifying column with adjustable bubble plates to increase the reflux rate and maximize the copper contact. This removes unwanted flavours, creating a clean, smooth spirit. The result is a fruity twist on a classic London Dry that's smooth enough to sip neat, but Emily also recommends serving Roundwood with plenty of ice, a quality Indian tonic water, orange peel and a sprig of thyme.

Roundwood have started offering Gin Discovery sessions (top left). You learn about how Roundwood Gin is produced and have a tutored tasting. Also watch out for their gin wagon (right) at shows and festivals around the country.

The Newmarket Gin at Bedford Lodge Hotel and Spa

Newmarket, Suffolk
Distillery and bar

ESSENTIAL INFORMATION

Key botanicals (The Newmarket Gin):
juniper, coriander, orange, wild chive, orchid petal, alfalfa, wild horseradish, bay leaf, almond, assorted wildflowers

Output: approximately 756 bottles a year

Location: Bedford Lodge Hotel & Spa, Bury Road, Newmarket, CB8 7BX

Telephone: 01638 663175

Email: info@thenewmarketgin.co.uk

Website: www.thenewmarketgin.co.uk

Facebook: www.facebook.com/thenewmarketgin

Instagram: @bedfordlodgehotelspa

Opening hours:
Roxana Bar
Lunch: Monday-Saturday 1200-1430
          Sunday 1230-1430
Dinner: Monday-Sunday 1830-2130

Other reasons to go: National Horseracing Museum, Bill Tutte Memorial, Newmarket's famous racecourses

Originally produced for Bedford Lodge Hotel & Spa, the Newmarket Gin (bottom left) was launched at the Gin Guild's Ginposium in June 2016 on the 350th anniversary of horse racing at Newmarket.

It is made using a double shot method in a copper pot still. The botanicals are steeped in English grain spirit, distilled to make vodka, which is then re-distilled to make a base for the gin. Alfalfa – one of the more unusual botanicals – is used not just for its mild nutty flavour but for its connection to horse racing – it's fed to Newmarket's thoroughbred racehorses.

In honour of the 350th anniversary, the bottle also has a handmade leather collar with a ribbon tag in the Newmarket stripe made by local saddlery Gibsons, to resemble riding tack. At the top of the label there is one horses in movement racing in the 2000 Guineas, and the label is in the style of a vintage betting slip.

In 2021, The Newmarket Gin expanded its collection with the addition of its flavoured Rhubarb gin (left bottle). Following the original recipe, it uses natural rhubarb juice and is a smooth, delicate gin The original Squire's Reserve is £55, and the Rhubarb is £57. You can find the gin at the Bedford Lodge Hotel & Spa.

Bullards Gin and The Anchor Distillery

Norwich

Distillery, gin school and bar

ESSENTIAL INFORMATION

Key botanicals (Bullards London Dry Gin):
juniper, coriander, liquorice, cardamom, cassia bark, black pepper, orange peel, lemon peel, tonka bean
Output: 20,000 bottles a year
Location: 24 Cattle Market Street, Norwich, NR1 3DY
Telephone: 01603 928585
Email: hello@bullardsspirits.co.uk
Website: www.bullardsspirits.co.uk
Facebook: www.facebook.com/bullardsgin
Instagram: @bullardsgin
Twitter: @BullardsGin

Opening hours:
Monday-Sunday 0900-2300

Other reasons to go: Norwich Castle Museum and Art Gallery, Norwich Cathedral

The Bullards brand was originally established in 1837, producing beer and spirits for over a hundred years, until production ceased in the late 1960s. Some 50 years later Russell Evans, who worked with Bullards in his youth, wondered what had become of it. He discovered that no one owned the brand, so he bought it, invested in a 120-litre still and opened The Ten Bells pub in 2015, resurrecting Bullards with a focus on gin. He brought in Craig Allison for his knowledge of the industry – he had a background of running bars around the world and launched Norwich's first Gin Palace in 2013. Keen to stand out from the crowd, Craig liked the idea of incorporating the vanilla and marzipan flavours of the tonka bean into the recipe.

The rest was left in the capable hands of head distiller, Peter Smith, who had just completed an internship at The Cotswolds Distillery when he joined the Bullards team. Peter used his knowledge to build a London Dry recipe, experimenting with the botanicals until he found a combination that worked with tonka beans.

All of the botanicals are added to the base spirit 12 hours before distillation to extract as much flavour as possible. The product is then distilled for 12 hours in a unique 600-litre copper still to produce 60 litres of undiluted gin, which is then cut with water to a strength of 42.5% to create Bullards London Dry Gin (left).

Bullards also produce Strawberry and Black Pepper Gin (opposite, top right), made with fresh strawberries infused for 72 hours before distillation to give the gin its pink colour. Black pepper is added for warmth. Bullards recommend adding this to Prosecco for a refreshing cocktail.

Their third product is Old Tom Gin (right), created by Bullards distiller Rory Smith, whose mixology background enabled him to create a gin that could be used in cocktails or sipped neat. He added his own twist, introducing honey, mango and Demerera sugar to produce a caramel hue. Other botanicals include pink pepper, black pepper, cassia bark, grapefruit peel and vanilla. This is best served neat over ice, or with a quality tonic water.

The gins can be bought from their distillery and online shop, each costing £40 for a 70-cl bottle.

In August 2019, Bullards moved to The Anchor Distillery on Cattle Market Street in Norwich (top left). As well as frequent tours, they hold tasting masterclasses where you get a brief history of gin and the Bullards brand. You then learn to make a perfect serve with their three signature gins. They also hold a gin school, where you make your own recipe – visit the website for prices and booking information. There's an onsite gin bar where you can sample their latest experiments – as we went to press, they were working on a samphire and seaweed concoction, but other examples include a Cold Brew Coffee Gin and a Distilled Negroni Gin.

Norfolk Gin

Norwich, Norfolk
Distillery

ESSENTIAL INFORMATION
Key botanicals (Norfolk Gin): juniper,
   coriander, green cardamom, citrus peel,
   plus three secret ingredients
Output: 10,000-12,000 bottles a year
Location: Nowich, Norfolk
Telephone: 01603 559047
Email: jonathan@norfolkgin.co.uk
Website: www.norfolkgin.co.uk
Facebook: www.facebook.com/NorfolkGin
Instagram: @norfolk_gin

Opening hours:
not open to the public

Norfolk Gin was started in 2014 by husband and wife Jonathan and Alison Redding (bottom) in the kitchen of their home in Norwich. After leaving the army as a major in 2001, Jonathan worked in government and for local charities, watching the gin craze as it gathered momentum. Alison, also working in local government, shared Jonathan's passion for craft gin and together they set about researching gins, botanicals and investing £400 in ingredients to get the project underway.

They got advice from the craft gin community, and were heartened by its warmth, encouragement and enthusiasm. Soon they realised that while stills are beautiful, they are expensive too. Having sampled some excellent 'bathtub' gins they decided to try that approach. The botanicals are prepared by hand (never chopped or mashed) and slowly steeped in a neutral (bought-in) grain spirit imparting a subtle straw-like colour, resulting in an aromatic premium gin. Jonathan knows of two or three other UK gin makers using this supremely simple method, which nonethless takes time (several days) and care to introduce the botanicals in the right sequence.

They experimented with hundreds of flavour combinations, and with immersing the botanicals for different lengths of time. Friends and family came to many a tasting session, until everyone agreed on the final recipe (number 55 out of 56) and the signature taste was established.

They launched in 2015, with their first retail outlet at Harper Wells, the Norwich wine merchant. The first batch of 15 bottles sold out in three days, so a waiting list was started.

Demand soon outgrew the couple's kitchen, so they set up a gin studio in their

back garden. Gin is still made there, with two other buildings – Matilda the English Shepherd Hut and Jennifer the bottling shack (above) – also allowing production to expand.

They see Norfolk Gin as appealing to today's gin drinkers while also respecting the past, with a traditional herbaceous flavour, like genever, alongside a gentle sweetness typical of Old Tom. Juniper and herb aromas are balanced with a touch of spice, sweetness and citrus for smooth, easy drinking.

They keep the full recipe secret but say that of the seven botanicals, two are grown by Jonathan in the garden. Croatian juniper, green cardamom and fresh lime are key, complemented by the secret combination of herbs.

The distinctive handcrafted Wade Ceramics bottle (opposite, top) is considered by many too pretty to bin: people like to re-use their empties, or turn them into lamp bases. Empties can be topped up at Reno Wine in Wymondham and the Jarrold department store in Norwich city centre, where a handcrafted iron refilling machine has been installed.

Alison and Jonathan still measure, pour, fill, seal and label every bottle before manning their Morgan three-wheeler, electric powered BMW i3 or Renault Twizy to deliver bottles in person (right).

For a list of stockists, see the website.

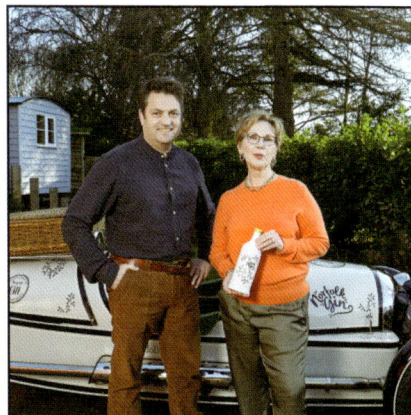

Suffolk Gin and Distillery

Sudbury, Suffolk
Distillery

ESSENTIAL INFORMATION

Key botanicals (Suffolk Dry Gin): juniper coriander, liquorice, cassia bark, cinnamon, citrus, plus four secret ingredients

Output: 1,200 bottles a year

Location: 38 Long Pastures, Glemsford, Sudbury, CO10 7SS

Telephone: 01787 280958; 07387 561871

Email: sales@suffolkdistillery.co.uk

Website: www.suffolkdistillery.co.uk

Facebook: www.facebook.com thesuffolkgin

Instagram: @thesuffolkgin

Twitter: @thesuffolkgin

Opening hours: not open to the public

Gary Wilkinson worked for large corporate distillers for most of his career. He had qualified as an applied chemist and in various roles was involved in cutting-edge distillation and botanical extraction techniques.

Like many a would-be craft gin maker wanting to quit the rat race, he saw the craft gin craze an opportunity and went for it – perhaps encouraged by his wife who had a good job and supported them both through the first months of debt and no pay. Like many another gin maker, he didn't regret his decision because although well paid (plus company car) he had no job satisfaction.

Now he does, but the catch is having to do everything in the business from paying bills to marketing, warehousing packing and dealing with HMRC.

He says his main gin, Suffolk Dry (left-hand bottle), is a homage to his home county, which he loves, and its climate. He describes the gin as 'an honest, traditional juniper-led dry gin, upfront on the juniper but then developing a dry citrus character' – with mellow spicy elements. The finish is fresh and fruity 'ending in a crescendo of sweet liquorice and warm spice, with a long lingering floral, citrus heady mix of ripened, intense berries.'

He also produces a Navy Strength (57% – right-hand bottle): 'think blustery seaside walks and crisp winter evenings followed by a nightcap by the fire,' enthuses his website. He also makes mandarin and cranberry (middle bottle); strawberry & cucumber and rhubarb gins.

Batch Gin and Batch Brew Ltd

Burnley, Lancashire
Distillery

ESSENTIAL INFORMATION

Key botanicals (Batch Signature Gin):
juniper, coriander, cardamom, cinnamon,
dried orange peel, nutmeg, allspice,
cloves, lemongrass, frankincese, myrrh

Output: not disclosed

Location: Unit 10 Habergham Mill, Coal
Clough Lane, Burnley, BB11 5BS

Telephone: 01282 701473

Email: info@batchbrew.co.uk

Website: www.batchbrew.co.uk

Facebook: www.facebook.com/BatchBrew

Instagram: @batchdistillery

Twitter: @batchdistillery

Opening hours:
Monday-Friday 0900-1700

Other reasons to go:
Towneley Art Gallery and Museum,
Gawthorpe Hall National Trust, Singing
Ringing Tree sculpture, Thompson Park

Phil Whitewell started his career in the drinks industry by producing craft beers for bars and restaurants around Hampshire. With the market becoming saturated, he was looking for a new venture and a trip to Madrid in 2012 exposed him to Spain's rich gin culture. Craft gin was just taking off in the UK, so he turned his hand to distilling. In November 2012, Phil received a distiller's license and started on the recipe for what he claims to be Lancashire's first gin.

He pulled a recipe off the internet and taught himself to distil – having no previous experience, he combined infusion with vapour infusion (page 28), a method he thought to be the norm. This turned out to be a happy mistake, and is one of the things that makes Batch Gin unique.

Production initially took place in Phil's nephew, now head distiller, Ollie's basement in Burnley, with only 40 bottles produced at a time. Ollie was a cobbler looking for a change, and Phil offered to teach him how to distil. They didn't want to make just another London Dry and while trawling through the website from which Phil buys botanicals, he stumbled across frankincense and myrrh. As it was Christmas, he liked the festive link and the spicy, earthy flavours the ingredients brought to the gin. Leaving the rest to his nephew, a year of experimenting followed before Ollie found the right balance of flavours.

Batch Signature Gin (left) was launched at a local gin festival in 2015 and Ollie's local pub was one of the first to stock it. It quickly gained notoriety, orders started coming in from abroad and they soon outgrew the basement, moving into a renovated mill with more space to welcome visitors. They commissioned a new stainless

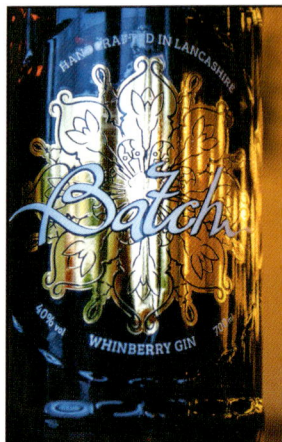

steel still, Adrian, with a 165-litre capacity and copper bubble plates (see Roundwood Distillery on page 119), giving them tight control over temperature and quality. They also have four smaller (25-litre capacity) stills to hand: Tom, Dick, Harry and The Other One.

Each run produces around 240 70-cl bottles of well balanced gin, good enough to sip neat. For a perfect serve, try a quality tonic water with lime peel and a crushed frozen raspberry to emphasize the orange flavour.

With new premises came new flavours – the first was Whinberry Gin (top right), the local term for bilberry which grows in the area. Bilberries are steeped in the Signature Gin and aged in former Cognac barrels. They also produce Batch Industrial Strength Gin (top left), their take on a Navy gin which pays homage to the industrial history of Burnley. This is less spicy and more juniper-led than the Signature Gin and is best served with a quality tonic, sage and dried apricots.

At present, the gins can be bought from their online shop, which also offers regularly-changing special deals on experimental gins.

Divine Spirits

Holmfirth, Yorkshire
Distillery

ESSENTIAL INFORMATION

Key botanicals (Divine London Dry Gin):
juniper, coriander seeds, liquorice,
cardamom, cubeb berries, grains of
paradise, orange peel, cassia bark,
cinnamon

Output: not disclosed

Location: Holme Valley, Yorkshire, HD9

Telephone: 07843 255876

Email: social@divinegin.com

Website: www.divinegin.com

Facebook: www.facebook.com/Gindivine

Instagram: @divinegin

Twitter: @gindivine

Opening hours:
Monday-Saturday by appointment only

Other reasons to go: Holmfirth vineyard,
historic Picturedome cinema, Summer
Wine Festival (seasonal)

Divine Gin comes from the Holme Valley in Yorkshire. Its makers call themselves R2 Distillers Ltd, R2 representing Ray and Rachel. The idea for their gin brand came to them while at a 4th of July party in 2014. Some time after, Ray decided to enrol on a distilling course. The duo then bought their first 50-litre still and set to work.

They tried out 36 recipes over the years, distilling each botanical individually to fully understand its taste. The result: Divine's signature London Dry Gin, which had a flavour profile that hit right across the palate. The initial sweetness from juniper develops into invigorating peppers followed by lingering spices. This is a genuine family-grown business, with every stage of production completed in house.

R2 soon realised that their Divine brand was as important as its unique, smooth flavour. They went back to the drawing board and incorporated wings into the initial Divine bottle design as a reference to their meeting whilst serving in the Royal Air Force. The gold colour gives it a luxurious, stand-out feel.

In 2022 they rebranded again, with a feather texture bottle and large stopper, which when opened releases the sweet juniper and peppers combined with spices inside. Their other gins include the Divine Raspberry Gin, their Navy Strength Gin, their Vodka and Coffee Liqueur.

Fairham Gin

Penwortham, Lancashire
Distillery

ESSENTIAL INFORMATION

Key botanicals (Signature Edition):
juniper, coriander seeds, cinnamon, pink grapefruit, lemon, clementine, guava, kumquat, physalis

Output: not disclosed

Location: Heaton Street, Lancashire, PR25 2ZH

Telephone: 07548 342472

Email: sales@no1fairhamgin.com

Website: www.no1fairhamgin.com

Facebook: www.facebook.com/FairhamGin

Instagram: @fairhamgin

Twitter: @FairhamGin

Opening hours:
not currently open to the public

Ellis McKeown and Liam Stemson (opposite, top left), the duo who make up Fairham Gin, can claim to be among two of the UK's youngest distillers at 24 and 25. They wanted to create a craft gin that would be true to traditional values but contemporary and unique to their brand. Their gins are juniper led, but use other botanicals to enhance the flavour.

Their Signature Edition (below) uses kumquat, physalis, guava and kaffir lime. It was released in April 2021 after 12 months of experimentation – and the result is a complex, smooth, dry gin with a fresh citrus taste.

They developed the recipe using a three-litre still in a Penwortham outbuilding on Fairham Avenue – which gave the gin its name – then moved to a small unit in Lancashire and purchased the 60-litre copper pot still that they operate today. Their batches are no more than 50 bottles, and their Dry Lancashire Gin is distilled via the one-shot method through vapour infusion; the botanicals sit in a copper basket in the column above the still's belly. Every process has been researched to deliver the best results, with the two distillers opting for a 45% ABV on their gins as standard and cutting out the chill filtration stage before bottling – meaning that you will notice a pearlescent haze to the gin when it's chilled in your glass.

They give their gins titles rather than flavour names to emphasise their big juniper flavours. In November 2021 they added Ochre Edition to the portfolio, their take on a spiced orange gin. This gin won a coveted three stars at the Great Taste Awards in 2022. It has tart juniper, fresh orange and sweet clementine flavours, backed with

layers of carefully blended spices. The range has been awarded accolades from industry-leading judges, with, they hope, more to come in the future.

As new distillers Ellis and Liam wanted to put their eco-friendly values to the fore. Since July 2021, each 70-cl bottle sold by Fairham Gin has bought a tree sapling for the Ribble Rivers Trust. The trees planted in Lancashire by this partnership will create new woodlands for people and wildlife to enjoy, and help to reduce carbon in the atmosphere. Ellis and Liam aim to become carbon negative after they have achieved their goal to open a distillery in the heart of Penwortham.

Hogarths

Preston, Lancaster
Bar

ESSENTIAL INFORMATION
Key botanicals (Willie Hogarth Old Tom Gin): juniper, coriander, liquorice, cardamom, citrus
Output: 140 bottles a year
Location: 140 Church Street, PR1 3BU
Telephone: 01772 253010
Email: info@ambertaverns.co.uk
Website: www.ambertaverns.co.uk/pub/hogarths-preston
Facebook: www.facebook.com/HogarthsPreston
Instagram: @hogarthspreston

Opening hours:
Sunday-Wednesday 1100-2300
Thursday 1100-2400
Friday-Saturday 1100-0100

Other reasons to go: Avenham and Miller Parks, Ribble Steam Railway and Museum, Harris Museum (Art Gallery and Library), Brockholes, 45 West Distillers Bar and Bottle Shop

Hogarths, named after satirical artist William Hogarth, are the winners of Best Multiple Gin Bar at the Think Gin Awards. Hogarths is a collection of Victorian-styled gin palaces offering the perfect mix between traditional town centre pubs and modern cocktail bars. The décor is themed around the classic Gin Palace and their mission is simply to serve great gin and cocktails in beautiful, relaxed surroundings. Each bar stocks over 80 varieties of gins and even the most experienced enthusiast is likely to find something new.

In addition to the extensive range of gins available, Hogarths offers their own small batch varieties – Hogarth's London Dry and Hogarth's Old Tom, developed with the fantastic Union Distillers (page 104). The London Dry has a subtle hint of vanilla and is best served with plenty of ice, Fever-Tree tonic water and a cucumber slice or citrus fruit. Their signature gin, Old Tom, is slightly sweeter with a liquorice taste, and best served with ice, Fever-Tree tonic, and an orange twist. They also produce Rhubarb, Strawberry and Vanilla and Sloe gins, as well as two gin liqueurs: passion fruit and bubblegum.

Their menus are carefully curated, recommending 'perfect serves' created specifically to showcase the best blend of botanicals, mixers and garnish for your gin. They offer a range of gin trees and a gin tray tasting experience, with something for every discerning customer.

They have locations all over the country, with new outlets planned for the future. Head to your nearest to unwind with the perfect serve of your choice.

Fynoderee Distillery

Ramsey, Isle of Man
Distillery

ESSENTIAL INFORMATION

Key botanicals (Fynoderee Manx Dry Gin):
juniper, elderflower, pink grapefruit,
lemon, lemon thyme, rosemary

Output: 16,000-20,000

Location: Parsonage Road, Ramsey, Isle of
Man, IM8 2EE

Telephone: 01624 812756

Email: teamfyn@fynoderee.com
bookings@fynoderee.com

Website: www.fynoderee.com

Facebook: www.facebook.com/Fynoderee

Instagram: @fynodereedistillery

Twitter: @fynoderee_iom

Opening hours:
Check website for tour times and seasonal
bar and shop opening times. Bespoke
tours are possible by arrangement.

Other reasons to go: The Fyn Bar (the
distillery's own feature cocktail bar),
Manx Electric Railway's northern terminus,
Ramsey's town centre shops, restaurants/
cafes and historic quayside

The only distillery in the guide based on the Isle of Man, a world UNESCO biosphere, Fynoderee is dedicated to premium spirits with Manx roots.

Husband-and-wife team Paul and Tiffany distill unique blends with Manx-grown, hand-foraged botanicals. As knowledgeable gin drinkers, they were frustrated that there was no small-batch gin producer on the island, whose environment is so ideal for producing quality ingredients.

After reading articles on the re-introduction of juniper to the Isle of Man by the Manx Wildlife Trust and a chance meeting with a master distiller, they took the plunge and formed the Fynoderee Distillery, launching their first 'seasonal' Fynoderee Manx Dry Gin in November 2017. Since then, the distillery has launched its Elder Shee range, using Elderflower as the key botanical. They have also ventured into vodka and rum.

An ancient Manx folk tale, *Kitty Kerruish and The Fynoderee*, is based in Glen Auldyn where the last juniper tree was said to have grown and where juniper has now been re-introduced. An Elfin prince was turned into the Fynoderee – half man, half goat – by the King of the Elves as punishment for falling in love with Kitty, a mortal girl. Legend has it that when paid with food and drink, the Fynoderee helps farmers with harvests, fishermen with nets and distillers with foraging and distilling.

For a perfect serve, pour a double shot (5 cl) over ice with premium tonic water. Garnish with (in spring) grapefruit, fresh rosemary or thyme; (in summer) fresh strawberry, raspberries or cucumber; (in autumn) apple or blackberries; (in winter) a twist of orange peel and a cassia quill.

Locksley Distilling Co. Ltd

Sheffield, South Yorkshire
Distillery

ESSENTIAL INFORMATION

Key botanicals (Sir Robin of Locksley
   Distilled Gin): juniper, coriander,
   liquorice root, cassia, dandelion, pink
   grapefruit, elderflower
Output: 20,000 bottles a year
Location: Unit 20C-1 Portland Works,
   Randall Street, Sheffield, S2 4SJ
Telephone: 0114 2490359
Email: info@locksleydistilling.com
Website: www.locksleydistilling.com
Facebook: www.facebook.com/
   sirrobinoflocksleygin
Instagram: @locksleydistilling
Twitter: @locksleystill

Opening hours:
Monday-Friday 0900-1700
Tours, tastings and gin-making classes on
   Wednesday, Friday, Saturday, Sunday by
   booking only

Other reasons to go: Sheffield Botanical
Gardens, The Peak District National Park

Locksley have been distilling premium spirits since 2013, with Sir Robin of Locksley Distilled Gin as their flagship product. It is a smooth-sipping gin that needs no mixer (although it's delicious in a G&T). Since then, their small but passionate team have been bringing the unexpected to the world of spirits. Never happy to give you a tipple that you can find elsewhere, the team thrives on finding a unique twist to make all their products quirky and memorable.

When pink gins exploded on to the craft gin scene, owner and distiller John refused to just chuck some berries into a product they already had. His wife, Cynthia, tried different flavour combinations until she hit on something that she loved. Thus, the Real Raspberry and Cardamom version was born, which surprises the discerning palate with a savoury, almost dry gin hidden in a pink gin – something which is usually sweet.

The third product of the distillery's core range is similarly unique. John decided he wanted to combine two old styles of gin together in one bottle. The result is their VSOT – Navy Strength, Very Special Old Tom Gin – with sweetness and strength memorably balancing each other.

The distillery is unpretentious and humble, striving for top quality and fair products.

Trippets Lounge Bar

Sheffield, South Yorkshire

Bar

ESSENTIAL INFORMATION
Location: 89 Trippets Lane, S1 4EL
Telephone: 01142 762930
Email: trippetsloungebar@hotmail.com
Website: www.trippetsloungebar.co.uk
Facebook: www.facebook.com/TrippetsBar
Instagram: @trippetsloungebar

Opening hours:
Thursday 1600-2230
Friday-Saturday 1200-2300
Sunday 1200-1600

Other reasons to go: Sheffield Cathedral,
Winter Gardens, Millennium Galleries

A stone's throw from Sheffield Cathedral and the City Hall, this independent jazz bar has become something of a landmark since it opened in 2015. Trippets Lounge Bar stocks 89 gins from around the world. Why 89 gins? Because they're based at 89 Trippets Lane. Their stock ranges from local gins produced by the Locksley Distillery, to Canaima Gin from Venezuela, back to Barra Gin (used to make their exceptionally good Dirty Martini). They have a varied cocktail menu including

a selection of martinis, Negronis (classic & bianco), plus classic gin cocktails such as their Hanky Panky, Tuxedo, the Last Word and the more unusual Genever Black (above).

The beauty of this place is that you don't have to be a gin connoisseur to drink here, nor should you feel overwhelmed by the vast choice of gins – Debbie, the owner, and her bar staff know their stuff and have been known to offer tasting samples and spontaneous gin masterclasses to help you find what tickles your tastebuds.

The food is also a hit here – Carl, the chef, provides a small plate dining menu. There's a live jazz band on Thursday nights, as well as a Sunday Brunch.

As we went to press, Trippets had plans to reinstate their Autumn Gin Festival. Distillers are invited and there's a band – so be sure to look out for it.

True North Brew Co.

Sheffield, South Yorkshire
Distillery and gin school

ESSENTIAL INFORMATION

Key botanicals (Sheffield Dry Gin): juniper, cardamom, fennel, gentian root

Location: Sheffield City Centre, South Yorkshire

Telephone: 01142 808222

Email: lucy@truenorthbrewco.uk

Website: truenorthbrewco.uk/Sheffield-dry-gin

Facebook: www.facebook.com/sheffielddrygin

Instagram: @sheffielddrygin

Twitter: @sheffielddrygin

Opening hours:
Monday-Friday 0900-1700
Gin school by booking only

Other reasons to go: Sheffield Botanical Gardens, Crucible Theatre, the Peak District

Sheffield Dry Gin is True North Brew Co.'s award-winning, premium small-batch gin expertly crafted in hand-made copper pot stills imported from Portugal. The distillery combines locally-sourced ingredients with pure water from the Peak District to create a unique taste deriving from its surroundings.

Since launching Sheffield Dry Gin Original in 2014, they've developed a core range bursting with flavour. This includes their original dry, marmalade, strawberry and black pepper, raspberry and pomegranate, moorland berries, and rhubarb gins, as well as a few limited editions.

Ginthusiasts can spend a day discovering the history of their favourite tipple at their gin school, and use their favourite botanicals to create a unique bottle of gin under the guidance of an expert.

The company create truly 'northern' spirits by collaborating with local businesses, providing them with the opportunity to infuse their signature products into a limited-edition gin. For example, True North Brew Co.'s Old Tom Gin is made with Simpkins Liquorice Nipits, a much-loved traditional sweet of Sheffield. In 2022, the distillery joined forces with local Sheffield artist, Rob Lee, to create a special limited edition Celebration Gin, with a peel and reveal label, marking 30 years of True North Brew Co.

Their dedicated gin sales manager, Lucy, supplies pubs, bars and gin shops across the country. Order via their website, where you can also buy luxury Sheffield Dry Gin gift sets – perfect for special occasions.

Bakewell Gin and The Wirral Distillery

Spital, Wirral
Distillery

ESSENTIAL INFORMATION

Key botanicals (Bakewell Gin – bottom):
juniper, coriander, cardamom, almond,
raspberry, cherry, hibiscus
Output: 120,000 bottles a year
Location: Online only
Telephone: 01513 349784
Email: info@wirraldistillery.com
Website: available at www.mygin.co.uk
Facebook: www.facebook.com/
WirralDistillery
Instagram: @wirraldistillery
Twitter: @WirralDistiller

Opening hours: not open to the public

Wirral Distillery is in the grounds of Poulton Hall in an 18thC brewhouse on the NE side of the main house. The Poulton Lancelyn family settled here in the 12thC and legend has it that the grounds are haunted by the White Nun, an infamous ghost who was murdered in the 1700s when travelling from Liverpool to Chester Cathedral. The Poulton Lancelyn surname became Lancelyn Green in the 16thC, and the same family produced the writer Robert Lancelyn Green.

Wirral distils more than 50 unique gins using copper stills and the vapour extraction method (see page 28). The botanicals hang in muslin bags above the boiling liquid, producing a fresh, sulphate-free flavour. Sulphates can be released when botanicals are simply boiled.

The distillery claims to be the home of the original Bakewell Gin (White Peak produces a Bakewell Pud Gin – see page 92), which they recommend serving with a quality tonic water and a cherry.

Among the distillery's signature gins is Wirral Gin, made with bog myrtle which literally defines the place in which it's distilled. Wirral means 'myrtle corner' referring to bog myrtle which can be found in the area. Wirral also makes Violetta Parma Violet Gin (next page, top left), a purple, pearlescent, shimmering spirit – the first of its kind. Released in 2016, it uses natural flavours and colours. They recommend adding it to Prosecco. Along similar lines is Strawberry Candy Floss Gin, a pink gin best served with a quality tonic, lemonade and sliced strawberries.

Wirral's most popular edition is, however, Pink Dog Gin, which has a hint of rose and a soft pink hue, reminiscent of

Turkish Delight. It stole the show at the gin festival where it was launched in September 2016. Try it with a sliced strawberry, Fever-Tree tonic and plenty of ice, or peppercorns to bring out its spicy flavour.

The distillery is currently closed to the general public, and their shop has moved online. You can buy Wirral Gin at www.mygin.co.uk.

Alnwick Gin and Northumberland Spirits

Alnwick, Northumberland
Distillery

ESSENTIAL INFORMATION

Key botanicals (Alnwick Gin): juniper, rosehip, lavender, fennel, plus seven secret ingredients

Output: 10,000+ bottles a year

Location: Blacksmiths Hall, Rock, Alnwick, NE66 3SB

Telephone: 01665 579100

Email: office@northumberlandspirit.co.uk

Website: www.alnwickgin.co.uk

Facebook: www.facebook.com/ RealAlnwickGin

Instagram: @alnwickgin

Twitter: @NorthlandSpirit

Opening hours:
Monday-Friday 0900-1700

Other reasons to go: Alnwick Castle, The Alnwick Garden, Bailiffgate Museum

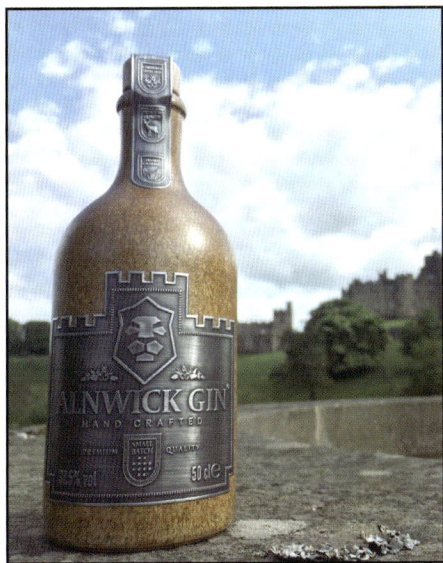

Neil Osborne discovered his love for gin after his wife introduced him to the classic G&T, which thereafter became his favourite summer nights tipple. It reminded him of his grandfather, who once allowed him into his garden shed where he made beer, cider and gin – illegally. Forty-five years later, Neil was coming to the end of a job contract and looking for his next venture, when he had a light-bulb moment – to reproduce his grandad's gin, which had been popular with locals all those years ago.

He founded The Northumberland Spirit Company in June 2016, and spent many months of trial and error to get as close to his grandfather's recipe as possible. After being sampled and approved by friends and locals, Alnwick Gin (below) was finally launched in October 2016.

The reaction was so positive, that he had to set up a website and online shop within days to meet demand. He sold his first batch – 200 bottles – in three days. Within the first couple of weeks, he realized he would need a bigger premises than the garden shed so bought two garages where he continued production. In July 2017, The Northumberland Spirit Co. moved to their current premises at Blacksmiths Hall.

As well as Alnwick Gin, they also produce three gin-based fruit liqueurs (next page, bottom right): Rhubarb and Strawberry, Lime and Ginger, and Raspberry and Vanilla, plus a Sloe Gin (next page, top right). In 2019, they released Firestorm Gin made with ten botanicals including juniper, lemon, lime, apple, lavender and horseradish. The name is a combination of the distillery's history as a blacksmiths hall and the subtle heat that comes from the horseradish. They also

produce bespoke, limited edition gins for several businesses and organizations.

Their unique bottle for Alnwick Gin is particularly appealing: it is made of stone with a label made of pewter – a nod to Alnwick Castle and its history as the home of the Earls and Dukes of Northumberland.

Purple Ram Gin and Yorkshire Dales Distillery

Colburn, North Yorkshire
Distillery

ESSENTIAL INFORMATION

Key botanicals (Purple Ram Gin): juniper, pink grapefruit peel, local honey, plus four secret ingredients

Output: not disclosed

Location: Unit 7C, Easton Way, Colburn, Catterick Garrison, DL9 4GA

Telephone: 01748 518070

Email: helloram@yorkshiredalesdistillery. com

Website: www.yorkshiredalesdistillery.com

Facebook: www.facebook.com/ yorkshiredalesdistillery

Instagram: @yorkshiredalesdistillery

Twitter: @homeoftheram

Opening hours:
Monday-Friday 0900-1700

Other reasons to go: Bolton Abbey Estate, Bolton Castle, Dales Countryside Museum, Black Sheep Brewery

Tony Brotherton and his wife Sarah founded the family-run Yorkshire Dales Distillery in April 2016, with the aim of producing spirits using locally sourced ingredients and providing jobs for the long-term unemployed, such as veterans and ex-offenders. In November of that year, they moved the distillery into a former wine warehouse. Tony served in the Royal Artillery for 18 years and later studied for his Master's in Brewing and Distilling at Heriot-Watt University to revitalize his long-term passion for distilling – he was once caught brewing beer at school.

Yorkshire Dales' first product, Purple Ram Gin, was released in February 2017. Initially, distillation took place on a 30-litre still, producing 50 bottles per run. A year on, demand saw Tony invest in another still ten times the size of the original, which produces 80 cases of gin per batch. Purple Ram is a classic London Dry-style gin with floral, citrus and honey flavours, best served with basil and a wedge of grapefruit over ice.

Their second offering was Desert Ram 'Army Strength' Gin, a nod to Tony's time in the army. Made with bitter orange, rose and cardamom, this works well with a grapefruit slice and ice. Their third gin is another dry gin: Wild Ram 'Yorkshire Berry' Gin, made with locally sourced gooseberries, redcurrants, blackcurrants and heather. All their spirits are quadruple distilled using the vapour infusion method before they are cut with natural mineral water from the Dales.

The distillery offers bookable group tours for a minimum of ten people, including a two-hour tour of the distillery with a tasting session, including one

signature serve of your choice.

In addition to their core 'Ram' range, Yorkshire Dales also produces a niche collection of gins – their YD range (below). These include Honeyed Rhubarb Gin, Bramble Berry Gin, and Strawberry and Thai Basil Gin. All products, including a vodka and rum, can be bought direct from their distillery or the online shop.

Masons of Yorkshire Distillery

Bedale, North Yorkshire
Distillery, shop and bar

ESSENTIAL INFORMATION

Key botanicals (Masons Yorkshire Gin):
    juniper, coriander, cardamom, citrus peels,
    fennel seed, bay leaf, Szechwan pepper
Output: not disclosed
Location: Trinity Place, Conygarth Way,
    Leeming Bar, DL7 9EE
Telephone: 01677 426467
Email: info@masonsyorkshire.com
Website: www.masonsyorkshiregin.com
Facebook: www.facebook.com/
    MasonsYorkshireGin
Instagram: @masonsofyorkshire
Twitter: @MasonsGin

Opening hours:
Monday-Friday 0900-1730
Saturday-Sunday open for events only

Other reasons to go: Thorp Perrow, St
Gregory's Church, The Bridge Gallery

Ella Carr writes: It was only a matter of time before Yorkshire, a county with a robust sense of itself, brought forth a representative Yorkshire gin. In 2013, Karl and Cathy Mason (next page, bottom right) – gin enthusiasts with no prior knowledge of the industry – single-handedly revived the Yorkshire distilling tradition when they set out to make an artisan, craft-made gin that stood out from the crowd.

Their Original Masons Gin (next page, top middle bottle) was launched on World Gin Day that same year, from their small distillery in picturesque Bedale. Fast forward to 2019 and Masons has grown into one of the UK's leading premium craft gin distillers.

Despite Masons' growth, the essence of its gin remains the same as when it started: all the gins are distilled in copper stills in small batches, using a traditional, London Dry, slow distillation method and just the right balance of botanicals to create a distinctive gin. Every batch is taste tested, both neat and with tonic, to ensure they meet high standards.

Their core gins are Original, Lavender (next page, top right bottle), Tea (next page, top left bottle), and Peppered Pear (next page, bottom left), while 'Special Edition' gins have included Slow Distilled Sloe, and Steve's Apple. All use Yorkshire products, including, of course, Yorkshire Tea.

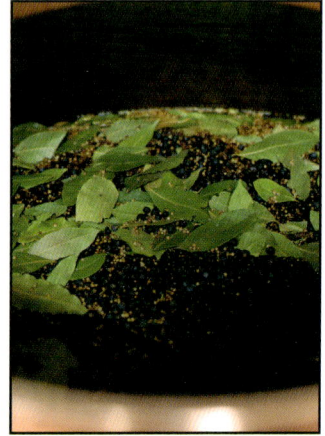

To best enjoy Masons gin, pair with premium tonic, plenty of ice and complementary garnish: try orange peel with the Original, lemon peel with the Tea edition and lime peel with Lavender. Alternatively, try the Lavender with ginger ale, or Tea with bitter lemonade.

Unfortunately, on the 2nd May 2019, the Masons Distillery was destroyed in a fire. They came back stronger in 2020, but turned their focus to online sales when the pandemic hit. Now they are back up and running, with tours and a shop at their new distillery.

Durham Gin and Distillery

Durham
Distillery

Durham Distillery was founded by Jon Chadwick (next page, middle), who was inspired by a trip to the USA's East Coast where he found there was a growing taste for gin that mirrored the craft beer movement in the UK. Using the redundancy money from his previous job in the NHS (in a team that spread awareness of the dangers of alcohol abuse) Jon decided to make his own gin. He and his then Master Distiller spent about a year developing a recipe and Durham Gin (below left) was launched with the opening of the distillery in 2014.

Head distiller Jess Tomlinson (next page, top left) uses a combination of pot distillation and vapour infusion (page 28). She crushes the juniper (above) by hand and adds it to Lily, their 400-litre copper pot still, along with the more robust botanicals, such as angelica and pink peppercorn. The botanicals are left to infuse in Durham spring water and pure grain spirit overnight before the coriander and orris root are added, and the mixture heated. The vapour produced is used to distil the more delicate botanicals such as elderflower, celery seed, cardamom and citrus peels, which sit in a basket at the top of the still. Distillation takes five to six hours, after which the head and tail of the run are removed (the tails are recycled in the production of their vodka – see bottom right, right-hand bottle). The

gin is cut with water to 40% to produce 300 bottles of London Dry style gin. Try it in a Negroni.

Jess also produces Strawberry and Pink Pepper Liqueur, made by soaking the peppercorns in Durham Gin for 24 hours before blending the spirit with fresh strawberry juice. This works well in a Strawberry Collins cocktail: add 50 ml of the gin to 25 ml of lemon juice, 10 ml of grenadine syrup and top with soda water, with lemon slices and cocktail cherries to garnish.

Each year, Jess produces a different Cask Aged Gin (right, left-hand bottle), rested for nearly 18 months in a combination of American Bourbon and Spanish Oloroso Sherry casks to produce a fruity, honeyed flavour with hints of vanilla and citrus zest. She produces just over a thousand bottles each year, and it's best served neat with ice. She also makes a Damson, Blackberry and Ginger Liqueur, a winter warmer made with Durham Gin. All the gins can be bought from the online shop.

Weetwood Distillery

Kelsall, Cheshire
Distillery

ESSENTIAL INFORMATION

Key botanicals (London Dry Gin): juniper, coriander, liquorice root, cardamom, cinnamon bark, cassia bark, bitter orange, sweet orange, lemon peel, blackcurrants,hops, caraway seed, ground almond, tellicherry pepper
Output: not disclosed
Location: The Brewery, Common Lane, Kelsall, Cheshire, CW6 0PY
Telephone: 01829 752377
Email: sales@weetwoodales.co.uk
Website: www.weetwoodales.co.uk
Facebook: www.facebook.com/ Weetwoodalesanddistillery
Instagram: @weetwoodcheshire
Twitter: @weetwoodales

Opening hours:
Monday-Thursday 0900-1700
Friday 0900-1630

Other reasons to go: Sandstone Trail, Eddisbury Way, Chester Folk Festival, Delamere Forest

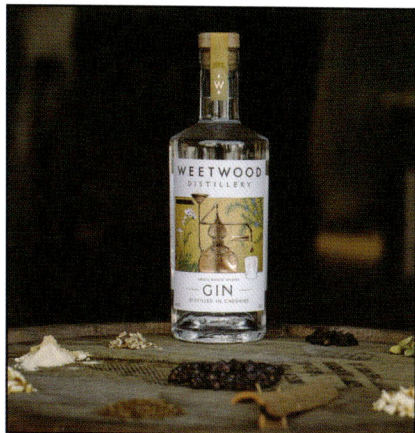

Weetwood Ales was established in 1992 in a barn in the hamlet of Weetwood in Cheshire. It was run as a brewery for many years by the original owners until they sold the business to family team Phil and Laura in 2014. They extended the buildings and set up Weetwood Distillery in 2018, which sits alongside the brewery. They purchased a custom-built Kothe still, and their first gin, a London Dry, was launched in October 2018 along with a triple-distilled Cheshire Vodka. They've since added Raspberry Gin and Apple Brandy to the range. Marmalade Gin has been launched which is made with marmalade from Mrs Darlington's – another Cheshire business. They also produce ready-to-drink spirit cans including a G&T and Rum, Lime and Ginger.

The whole production process takes place at the distillery – all the way through to bottling and labelling. The gins contain their own Weetwood Spirit – for which the barley is mashed in the brewhouse.

Another Weetwood enterprise is single malt whisky. This is made from spirit laid down over the past few years for maturation, with the first batch ready in autumn 2022. It's been subject to temperature fluctuations as it has matured – cold Cheshire winters and hot days in summer. The barrels are shaved and toasted, to provide a unique flavour and depth of colour.

Ribble Valley Gin Company

Longridge, Lancashire
Distillery and gin school

ESSENTIAL INFORMATION

Key botanicals (Little Lane Gin): juniper, nettles, heather, oak, meadowsweet, blackberries, pine

Output: not disclosed

Location: Little Ln, Longridge, Preston, PR3 3NS

Telephone: 01772 597791

Email: hello@ribblevalleygin.co.uk

Website: www.ribblevalleygin.co.uk

Facebook: www.facebook.com/ ribblevalleyginco

Instagram: @ribblevalleyginco

Twitter: @ribblevalleygin

Opening hours:
Monday-Friday 0900-1700

Other reasons to go: Lancashire Cycleway, Browsholme Hall, Holmes Mill, The Tolkien Trail

Justine and Luke Moyes (bottom left) were dedicated craft gin fans when they started Ribble Valley Gin in 2018, setting up in an outhouse – a former piggery dating back to 1888.

Their 130-litre still allows them to use either the maceration or the vapour infusion method, depending on which suits the botanicals best. They believe these processes give their gins a smooth and distinctive edge. They wanted their gins to reflect the beauty and character of the countryside surrounding them. For example, Little Lane Gin (opposite, top left), their hedgerow-inspired signature product, is rustic and uses ingredients directly from the area, including nettles, blackberries and pine (full list above left).

This is a genuine small batch operation, just the two of them overseeing every stage of the process from foraging to bottling and labelling.

The labels stand out for their charming wildlife illustrations featuring rabbits, butterflies, wild strawberries plus many other plants or animal inhabitants of field and fell. This is Lancashire, where the landscape is especially varied, with the fertile Ribble Valley giving way to moorland and steep Pennine hillsides (fells). Each label is carefully planned and features all the botanicals in the gin. They're the work of local artist Laura Brown whose studio is a fellside shed.

Including custom-made gins, the award-winning Ribble Valley range stood at eight gins when we went to press, and the illustrated labels, with their bright but not gaudy colours, give the collection a cheery, cohesive identity.

Try serving Little Lane with a slice of lime, a couple of blackberries and tonic water. For a sweeter drink, use an elderflower tonic.

Their fruity, floral Garden Party Gin, made with strawberries, wild thyme, honeysuckle, hibiscus and rose petals, could be the making of an impromptu outdoor gathering. Try serving with ice, strawberries and a sprig of thyme.

Cooper King Gin and Distillery

Sutton-on-the-Forest, York
Distillery and bar

ESSENTIAL INFORMATION

Key botanicals (Cooper King Dry Gin): juniper, coriander seed, green cardamom, lemongrass, lavender, honey

Output: 10,000 bottles a year

Location: The Old Stable, Stillington Road, Sutton-on-the-Forest, York, YO61 1EH

Telephone: 01347 808232

Email: info@cooperkingdistillery.co.uk

Website: www.cooperkingdistillery.co.uk

Facebook: www.facebook.com/cooperkingdistillery

Instagram: @cooperkingdistillery

Twitter: @ckdistillery

Opening hours:
Saturday 1200-1800

Other reasons to go: Castle Howard, York Bird of Prey Centre, the Yorkshire coast, York city centre

Yorkshire is becoming a hub for distillers. Cooper King is about 10 miles north of York, sitting between the Howardian Hills Area of Outstanding Natural Beauty and the rugged Yorkshire Dales National Park.

Cooper King was founded by Dr. Abbie Neilson, a biomedical scientist, and Chris Jaume, a chartered architect (both opposite, top left). The pair were inspired by distillers they visited on a trip to Australia and Tasmania, where they studied with Bill Lark, a prolific distiller.

The distillery takes its name from Chris' great-great-grandfather, who was a lieutenant colonel of the Royal Marine Artillery and traced his family history back to 1030 and the Pigot family in Yorkshire.

The distillery was built by Chris and Abbie with help from friends, family, and supporters. It is proud of its environmental credentials and sustainable spirits, running exclusively on renewable energy and recycling water and waste. It is also part of the '1% for the Planet' initiative, which means that 1 per cent of sales are used to plant trees in the Yorkshire Dales with their charity partner, Yorkshire Dales Millennium Trust. 20,000 square metres of new woodland was planted, offsetting 230 tonnes of carbon dioxide and improving the area's landscape and biodiverisity. They've

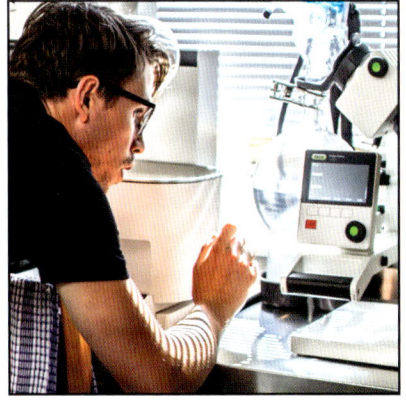

also planted juniper bushes at the distillery.

At the start of 2021, they announced production of what can claim to be England's first carbon-negative gins. They have also been invited to speak about their sustainability initiatives to members of EU parliament, at a distilling expo in London, a climate conference in Yorkshire, live on Sky News and BBC radio, and given a masterclass at York University. They're passionate about sharing their learnings to encourage progress within the industry.

Cooper King is currently open to the public on Saturdays, with guided tours taking place in the afternoon. Visitors can learn about making gin and whisky, bring back an empty bottle for a gin refill, and have a G&T or cocktail at the on-site bar. You can also stay overnight in the distillery's bed and breakfast.

The original Dry Gin (opposite, bottom), launched 2018, is produced using the vacuum distillation method with a spirit made from Yorkshire-grown wheat, locally-sourced lavender and honey from the distillery's own beehives. Recent collaborations include Earthly Spirits Gin with Selfridges and Discovery Gin with the London Natural History Museum, as well as a number of high-end restaurants.

Oro Gin and
The Distillery at Dalton

Dalton, Dumfries and Galloway
Distillery and bar

ESSENTIAL INFORMATION
Key botanicals (Oro Gin): juniper, cassia bark, malabar cardamom, lemon and orange peels, pink peppercorns, lemongrass and one secret ingredient
Output: 5,000-10,000 bottles a year
Location: The Distillery, Dalton, Dumfries, DG11 1DU
Telephone: 01387 840381
Email: info@theorogin.com
Website: www.orogin.co.uk
Facebook: www.facebook.com/theorogin
Instagram: @oro_gin
Twitter: @theorogin

Opening hours:
Tours available by appointment
Thursday and Friday 1200-1600
The Oro Bar
Monday-Thursday 1000-1800
Friday 1000-late
Saturday 1200-late
Sunday 1200-1800

Other reasons to go: Dumfries and Galloway Aviation Museum, Caerlaverock Castle

Oro Gin was launched in December of 2017 by the Clynick family, who wanted to create a gin based on scientific understanding of different flavour compounds and how they interact with each other. *Oro* is Spanish for gold and the bottle labels feature gold concentric circles to represent the atomic structure of the element.

The botanicals are macerated for 24 hours with a neutral grain spirit before being distilled using the one-shot method. Before they are cut with water, most London dry recipes are 70% after distilling. Oro Gin, however, is cut at a higher strength to ensure an even cleaner, purer spirit. It's then diluted to 43% with pure water.

The Clynicks also produce Oro V, using lavender as a smoothing agent. Try mixing this with an elderflower tonic and a slice of lemon. The Oro Bar at the distillery has a vast range of gins, as well as their core spirits and beers, and an ever-growing cocktail list, from the traditional to the experimental. There is also a pleasant courtyard and a conservatory for the warmer months.

Using scientific principles, Oro has developed a new Strawberry Gin, using an innovative extraction method to capture the natural flavours of British strawberries. It is one of the first of three new products which will form the brand's Nitro Collection. The Clynicks' innovative pressurised extraction method involves passing nitrogen into a pressure-stable vessel that contains Oro gin, Madagascan vanilla, Sri Lankan cracked black pepper, and British strawberries.

They can also design bespoke products for special occasions or businesses.

DeliQuescent and Rutherfords Micropub

Kelso, Scottish Borders
Distillery and bar

ESSENTIAL INFORMATION

Key botanicals (ChiQuiOui Gin): juniper,
   plus 11 secret ingredients
Output: not disclosed
Location: 38 The Square, Kelso, TD5 7HL
Telephone: 07803 208460
Email: rutherfordltd@googlemail.com
Website: www.rutherfordsmicropub.co.uk
Facebook: www.facebook.com/
   Rutherfordsmicropub.co.uk
Instagram: @rutherfordsmicropub_kelso

Opening hours:
Monday-Thursday 1500-2200
Friday 1500-2300
Saturday 1200-2300
Sunday 1200-2200

Other reasons to go: Floors Castle and
Gardens, Kelso Abbey, Roxburgh Castle,
Springwood Park

Rutherfords was opened by Debbie and Simon Rutherford in summer 2015 and can claim to be Scotland's smallest pub. They stock over 30 gins, including Isle of Harris, Gin Mare, plus their own creations.

They decided to make gin in October 2017, under the name DeliQuescent, which means 'becoming liquid', apt for a team of spirits producers specializing in unusual gins. Their signature taste, ChiQuiOui Gin, is juniper led with a kick of citrus, best served with a quality tonic and a wedge of pink grapefruit or orange.

Their Haggis Gin (below left), launched on Burns Night 2019. The gin's tagline is 'there's nothing offal in our gin', comically reassuring that only spices reminiscent of the Scottish savoury pudding are used, with luckily not a hint of meat. Haggis Gin works best with tonic and a citrus garnish, but Debbie and Simon also recommend serving it in true Scottish style – with Irn Bru.

They also produce seasonal gins: in winter 2018, they released Christmas Pudding, GINgerbread and GINgle Bells gins; in spring, a limited edition Hot Cross Bun Gin, using sultanas, citrus and spice.

The gins can be bought from Rutherfords micropub or their online shop. Debbie and Simon also sell their gins at Kelso's farmer's market on the third Saturday of most months from 10 am to 1.30 pm – check their website for dates.

Rutherfords offers an Afternoon G&T where three gins of your choice are served alongside cucumber sandwiches, manchego and parma ham, and handmade sweets – call or email to book.

Hills & Harbour Gin
Crafty Distillery

Newton Stewart, Dumfries and Galloway
Distillery and vistor centre

ESSENTIAL INFORMATION

Key botanicals (Hills and Harbour Gin):
  juniper, coriander seed, liquorice, orange
  peel, green sichuan pepper seed, bay
  leaf, mango, noble fir tree needle,
  bladderwrack seaweed

Output: 60,000 bottles a year

Location: Wigtown Road, DG8 6AS

Telephone: 01671 404040

Email: info@craftydistillery.com

Website: www.craftydistillery.com

Facebook: www.facebook.com/
  craftydistillery

Instagram: @craftydistillery

Twitter: @craftydistills

Opening hours:

January-March
  Tuesday-Saturday 1000-1730
  Tours from 1200 and 1500

April-December
  Monday-Saturday 1000-1800
  Tours from 1100, 1300 and 1500

Other reasons to go: Dark Skies Park,
Wigtown Book Festival, Newton Stewart
Museum, mountain biking

Newton Stewart, home town of Crafty's founder Graham Taylor, is in Dumfries and Galloway, the area sometimes loosely described as south-west Scotland, a generally unspoiled, out-of-the way corner of the British Isles. The town is known as the 'Gateway to the Galloway Hills' and with over 200 miles of coastline in the region, there's good reason that Crafty's gin is called Hills & Harbour (below left). They distil and bottle everything on site, and make their operation as green as possible. The distillery won Scottish Gin Distillery of the Year in 2020, and Best Scottish London Dry Gin in the World Gin Awards.

The wittily named Crafty Distillery (opposite, middle) is artfully dovetailed into the local tourist scene, providing what could be one of the most pleasant distillery experiences in southern Scotland. This is complemented by the visitor centre, a relaxing, airy stopping place with sprawling views over the Galloway Hills.

Combine the visit with a distillery tour plus a visit to the shop and you have a worthwhile expedition. The distillery also organizes the Gin Escape experience: join a guided exploration of the hills and coastlines to forage for botanicals, then head back to the distillery at the end of the day for a distillery tour, with two cocktails prepared by your guide from the ingredients you foraged.

And the gin? Also a deliberately commercial concept: Hills & Harbour, while being unique in its own right, was developed for the widest possible appeal. Graham and his friend Craig Rankin, distillery manager, say they tested 90 different recipes over 14 months to get the final formula, which they then made

in three different styles – one modern, one light and one sweet. Next they tested these on the general public and made final adjustments. The result, 'a vibrant, balanced and easy-drinking gin' is a deliberate move away from 'fussy niche gin' in order to turn new punters on to craft spirits. It's a 'grain-to-spirit gin' – no bought-in spirit is used.

The bottle recommends drinking Hills & Harbour however you like, but for a perfect serve put 25 ml in a tumbler with plenty of ice. Add 100 ml of Franklin's Tonic Water. Finish with a slice of fresh mango, which complements the mango used in distillation, but is also low in sugar and citrus. This allows the gin flavour to take centre stage.

Biggar Gin Co.

Biggar, South Lanarkshire
Distillery

ESSENTIAL INFORMATION
Key botanicals (Original Recipe Biggar Gin): juniper, cardamom, lemon peel, orange peel, nettles, rosehip, lavender
Output: not disclosed
Location: Biggar, South Lanarkshire, Scotland
Telephone: 01899 872122
Email: info@biggargin.com
Website: www.biggargin.com
Facebook: www.facebook.com/biggargin
Instagram: @biggargin
Twitter: @biggargin

Opening hours: not open to the public, visits by appointment only

Other reasons to go: Little Sparta, Culter Fell, Biggar and Upper Clydesdale Museum

This distillery was established by brothers Stuart and Euan McVicar in 2018, and it's no coincidence that they named it after Biggar, a prosperous town in the Southern Uplands that punches above its weight for the diversity of businesses located there – Biggar Gin Co. being a prime example.

Wittily describing their business philosophy as a 'Biggar mentality', the duo work from their distillery at the bottom of Tinto Hill. They make small batch, quality hand-crafted gins that mix tradition and innovation – combining small scale with big passion. They have adapted modern distilling methods to their own refined processes to create unique, delicious gin. The ingredients reflect the local landscape but the result also pays homage to traditional gin.

Their Original Recipe Biggar Gin is produced in batches of no more than 140, and was Winner in the London Dry Gin category at the Gin Guide Awards 2018. Serve with tonic and orange peel over ice.

The gin can be bought at the distillery, online, or from various shops, bars and restaurants around the country. They also offer distillery tours and tutored tasting sessions by appointment, and they operate a mobile Biggar Gin bar from a converted horsebox trailer.

beGIN

Glasgow
Bar

ESSENTIAL INFORMATION
Location: 383 Byres Road, G12 8AU
Telephone: 01413 416516
Email: beginbar@outlook.com
Website: www.beginglasgow.com
Facebook: www.facebook.com/
    beginglasgow
Instagram: @beginglasgow

Opening hours:
Sunday-Thursday 1530-0000
Friday-Saturday 1230-0100

Other reasons to go: Glasgow Necropolis,
Kelvingrove Art Gallery and Museum, Pollok
Country Park

Ella Carr writes: You have to applaud beGIN's commitment to gin. It hosts a roster of events to entice diehard gin heads as well as newbies. The bar holds around 100 gins (opposite, bottom left), with a special emphasis on Scottish and local gins (flowers are displayed in Garden Shed Gin bottles, a gin made by by two local rugby players in – you guessed – their garden shed). You can tailor your own G&T with a selection of garnishes and tonics, or opt for their perfect serve. If you're struggling which to choose, go for the Gin Flight: different gins themed The Bold, The Beautiful, The Best and Scottish. Membership of their Gin Club is free, giving you access to exclusive events such as Meet the Makers each month, and tastings.

Black walls and ceilings with pink inserts (apparently referencing the pink gin craze) make this a proper late night joint – speakeasy style. The staff, who personally gutted and re-did the place when it was bought in 2016, have added a touch of industrial chic, with copper pipe glass racks (next page, top left), purple lights and the odd copper still (next page, top right). At night, especially on weekends when DJs are brought in, the bar is rammed – the place to sample Glasgow's famous nightlife.

On my mid-week afternoon visit, the bar was significantly more sedate. I settled back with a Makar Scottish G&T – not my favourite, though I enjoyed the chilli garnish (next page, middle right). Perhaps

more exciting ones to try here include Hills & Harbour (see page 154), a grain-to-bottle variety recommended by the barman; Bakewell Gin, a spicy gin with hints of ground almond and cherry jam; and Four Pillars Bloody Shiraz, a deep purple, richly jammy gin hailing from Australia, made from Yara Valley Grapes.

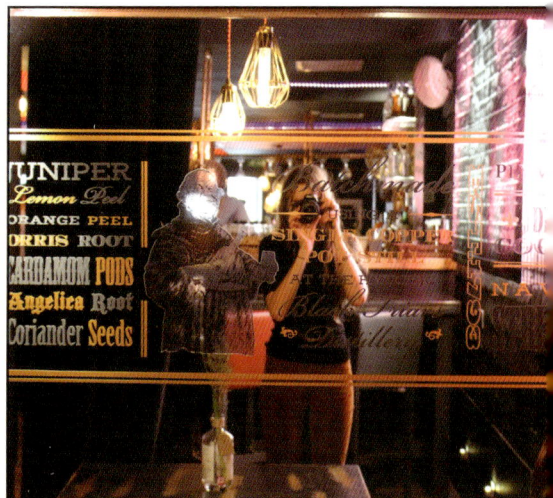

Crossbill Gin and Distillery

Glasgow
Distillery and gin school

ESSENTIAL INFORMATION
Key botanicals (Crossbill Gin): juniper,
  rosehip
Output: not disclosed
Location: Unit 1 BAaD, 54 Calton Entry,
  G40 2SB
Telephone: 0141 237 4664
Email: enquiries@crossbillgin.com
Website: www.crossbillgin.com
Facebook: www.facebook.com/CrossbillGin
Instagram: @crossbill_highland_distilling

Opening hours:
Monday-Friday 0900-1700

Other reasons to go: Kelvingrove Art Gallery
and Museum, Glasgow Cathedral, Riverside
Museum, Gallery of Modern Art

David Smith writes: Crossbill Gin's story began in 2012 in a converted shed on an estate near Aviemore, Scotland, a characterful location which was awarded Shed of the Year by Channel 4 in 2015.

In 2017, the distillery moved to a new home near Barras Market in the Trongate area of Glasgow, quickly transforming itself from a remote, rural distillery to a bustling urban one. The new home enables people to get to know the gin via the visitor centre and shop. This runs The Gin School course (below and opposite, top right) three times a week, offering participants an interactive session covering the distillery's background, spirit production, and how to impart flavour to spirits. You get a tutored tasting of Crossbill products, before making your own gin. Unusually for a gin school, the stills have vapour baskets, so you can also explore vapour botanical distillation.

Crossbill Gin is made using only two botanicals, and both are sourced from Scotland. Common juniper comes from the Cairngorms and, whilst this is the same variety that many other distilleries source from Tuscany and the Mediterranean, the differences in climate affect the character of the juniper. The Scottish berries are more aromatic and slightly lighter. The second botanical is rosehip: a plant that commonly grows near juniper and also works well in gin, adding its own resinous character.

Crossbill 200 is a special annual release: a vintage gin made from juniper berries harvested from a 200-year-old juniper bush and the rosehips growing around it.

In 2017, Crossbill teamed up with That Boutique-y Gin Company to produce 3D Juniper Gin, made using both green and purple juniper berries, juniper wood, and needles.

Pickering's Gin and Summerhall Distillery

Edinburgh
Distillery and bar

ESSENTIAL INFORMATION

Key botanicals (Pickering's Gin): juniper, coriander, cardamom, lemon, lime, anise, cloves, fennel
Output: 438,000 bottles a year
Location: Summerhall, Edinburgh, EH9 1PL
Telephone: 0131 290 2901
Email: enquiries@pickeringsgin.com
 tours@pickeringsgin.com
Website: www.pickeringsgin.com
Facebook: www.facebook.com/
 Pickeringsgin
Instagram: @summerhall_distillery

Opening hours:
Distillery Shop
Monday-Friday 0900-1700
Saturday-Sunday 1100-1800

Other reasons to go: Summerhall, The Queen's Hall, National Museum of Scotland

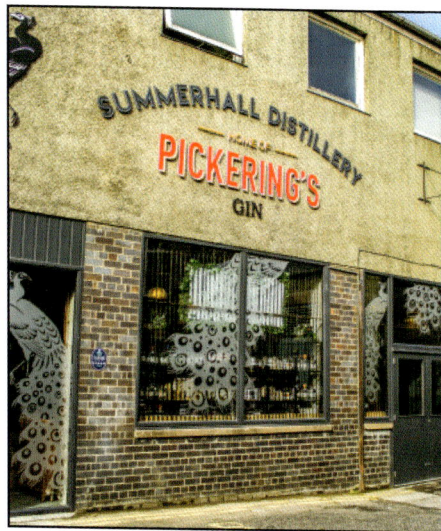

Ella Carr writes: Pickering's robust and spicy gin comes with an equally robust backstory – ever more important if a craft gin wants to stand out from the crowd. For starters, the distillery building (bottom left) was home to The Royal Dick Veterinary College of Edinburgh University between 1917 and 2011, and still bears the signs of 95 years of wear and tear – cat cages remain to this day stacked behind the stills, and until recently there were dog kennels in the bottling room. In 2012 Matthew Gammel and Marcus Pickering were brought in by the new owner – and founder of the abutting Royal Dick pub – to advise on transforming the rickety old building. Despite only ever distilling gins as a hobby, the pair spotted an opportunity.

The plan got legs when, in 2012, Marcus' father passed away and an old friend from India got in touch, offering condolences and bequeathing them his old family recipe for gin, handed down over generations. They received it in the post on a scrap of brown paper dated 1947, which now hangs framed in the distillery. The list of ingredients didn't come with any indication of quantity needed, so there was a laborious process of recipe development before they hit upon their 'red top' Pickering's Gin: a spicy yet smooth gin, with a hint of sweetness. In fact, the recipe listed nine pretty standard gin botanicals, such as coriander, fennel, cinnamon and star anise, but it's not a bad story, and the spice-oriented gin certainly deserves its 'Bombay style' tagline.

When Matt and Marcus launched Pickering's in 2014 they unwittingly made history, establishing the first exclusive gin distillery in Edinburgh for more than 150 years. They quit their day jobs and went

into distilling full time, turning Summerhall Distillery into a serious operation, producing 1,200 bottles a day. However, Pickering's is still bottled, corked and labelled on the premises, and the nicely shaped bottles made from quality glass – Matt was previously in the glass and crystal industry.

Because of the building and the gin's colourful history, Summerhall Distillery offers a compelling gin tour to visitors. It begins with a G&T in the eclectically decorated Royal Dick pub after which a spirited tour guide reels off the Pickering's story and makes introductions to their two stills, Gertrude and Emily (top right). Then you get a generous tasting of some of Pickering's favourites, including Pickering's Gin (called 'red top' for its wax seal), as well as Pickering's Original 1947 Gin, which follows the Bombay recipe even more precisely, and boosts the cardamon for an extra spicy kick. Next you'll try Pickering's Navy Strength (middle right) which comes with a little fluffy hat for the bottle, and a serious kick from its 57% strength. Afterwards, browse their extensive special editions, including Pickering's Gin with Scottish Botanicals and Pickering's sloe. During the festive season they also do Pickering's Gin Baubles (right) – one of their most popular items.

Secret Garden Gin and The Old Curiosity Distillery

Edinburgh

Distillery

ESSENTIAL INFORMATION

Key botanicals (Secret Garden Apothecary Rose Gin): juniper, coriander, winter savory, Apothecary rose

Output: 12,000 bottles a year

Location: 32A Old Pentland Road, Lothianburn, EH10 7EA

Telephone: 01312 856833

Email: info@theoldcuriosity.co.uk

Website: www.theoldcuriosity.co.uk

Facebook: www.facebook.com/ oldcuriositydistillery

Opening hours:

Monday-Friday 0900-1700

Saturday-Sunday bookings only

Other reasons to go: Edinburgh Castle, Royal Mile, Arthur's Seat, National Museum of Scotland

Ella Carr writes: As often happens, Hamish Martin's (opposite, middle) road to distilling gin was indirect and almost entirely accidental. He and his wife Liberty opened Secret Herb Garden in 2014 – a specialist herb nursery at the foot of the Pentland hills, just outside Edinburgh – which combined his passion for herbalism with her dream of opening a café and shop full of vintage furniture, wine and beer. It was only after the council threatened to revoke their wedding licence that they turned to gin as a way to fund their garden. Success quickly followed after the alcohol buyer for M&S tried one of their herbal gins at a wedding, and invited them to make the brand's British Rose Colour Changing Gin. The Old Curiosity Distillery's own range of colour-changing gins now includes Apothecary Rose (bottom left), Lavender and Echinacea (next page, bottom left), and Chamomile and Cornflower.

Gins may have started as a sideline, but Hamish's success as a distiller is not surprising. Before getting an MSc in herbology and opening his herb garden, he founded the acclaimed wine merchant Inverarity Vaults (sold on as Inverarity Morton). His gins stand out from the crowd because of their colour-changing properties, achieved with herbs which Hamish and Liberty grow, dry and harvest themselves.

The gin project is still relatively new, but Hamish has ambitious plans. At the back of the garden, rows of juniper plants are beginning to rear their heads for harvesting, while the 700 different types of herbs and flowers in the garden promise huge scope for flavour experimentation. As we went to press, tours and tasting classes were under way – see their website.

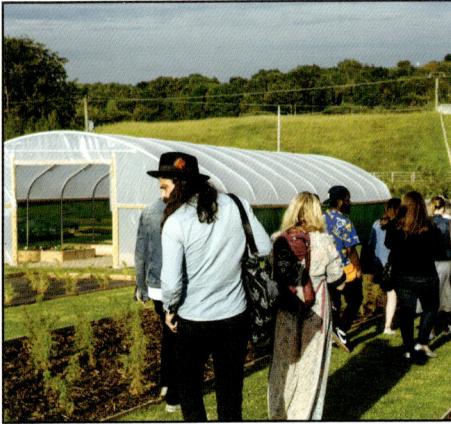

And, of course, it's not just about the gin. The 7.5 acres of herb garden (above), bordered by native hedgerows and a gentle stream, are a joy to visit in their own right. The Glasshouse – a wonderful canopied greenhouse furnished with antique furniture – is a great spot to eat seasonal food. Next to the herb drying room Hamish holds classes in herb-growing, bee-keeping, candle-making and foraging. To complete the bucolic scene, there's a baby animals pen, and pigs and geese wandering around freely. Children will be easily distracted while you enjoy the lovely herbal gin.

NB Distillery

North Berwick, East Lothian
Distillery

ESSENTIAL INFORMATION

Key botanicals (NB London Dry Gin):
    juniper, coriander seed, cardamom,
    cassia bark, grains of paradise, lemon
    peel

Output: not disclosed

Location: Halflandbarns, North Berwick,
    EH39 5PW

Telephone: 01620 894744

Email: sales@nbgin.com

Website: www.nbdistillery.com

Facebook: www.facebook.com/NBDistillery

Instagram: @nb_distillery

Twitter: @NB_Distillery

Opening hours:
Wednesday-Friday 1000-1600
Saturday 1000-1400

Other reasons to go: Scottish Seabird
Centre, Tantallon Castle, Coastal
Communities Museum, Seacliff Beach

NB Gin was launched in 2013 by husband and wife team Steve and Viv Muir, both lawyers. They secured a distiller's licence in 2011 and started experimenting in their kitchen, infusing botanicals and water in a pressure cooker to see which flavour combinations worked best. They enlisted the help of Charles Maxwell of Thames Distillers to help with the recipe, and once finalized, bought a proper still, which was later replaced by another, custom built in London. At first they distilled in batches of 100 litres, which has increased over the years as they've gained experience.

NB Gin is made from one hundred per cent British neutral grain spirit, using the one-shot distillation method (page 28). The result is a 42% London Dry style gin that works well with Fever-Tree tonic and a slice of lime. They also produce a Navy Strength Gin at 57%.

In April 2018, Steve and Viv moved the distillery to a small premises in North Berwick (where the brand gets its name). Here, they offer experiences such as Ginspiration Tour where you learn about their production process and the history of the brand. You also get a G&T and a tour of the distillery, and then you can relax upstairs in their tasting lounge for a 'flight' of a further four drinks. The tour lasts around an hour and a half from 5 pm, and costs £25. See the website for booking information.

McQueen Gin and Trossachs Distillery

Callander, Perthshire
Distillery

ESSENTIAL INFORMATION
Key botanicals (McQueen Highland Dry):
  juniper, lime, vanilla
Output: 250,000+ bottles a year
Location: The Barn, Upper Drumbane,
  FK17 8LR
Telephone: 01877 339929
Email: info@mcqueengin.co.uk
Facebook: www.facebook.com/mcqueengin
Instagram: @mcqueengin
Twitter: @McQueenGin

Opening hours:
Monday-Friday 1000-1700

Other reasons to go: Bracklinn Falls Bridge,
Loch Lubnaig, St Kessog's Church, The
Trossachs National Park

Some craft gins use a line-up of much the same ten botanicals, and can end up tasting pretty similar. When husband and wife Dale and Vicky McQueen (bottom left with First Minister Nicola Sturgeon) founded their brand in 2015, they wanted to stand out.

Alongside Highland Dry, their range also includes Citron; Five Chilli; and Colour Changing Gin (opposite, in order from bottom left), plus their fruity gins Blackcurrant and Raspberry, and Black Cherry and Vanilla. These flavours are pre-distilled instead of added. The result is pure and balanced rather than sickly or overbearing.

The Five Chilli in particular is fiery and warm, featuring some of the hottest chillies on the planet; Ghost, Carolina Reaper, Guajillo, Scorpion and Orange Habanero.

The title flavours of each gin are at once recognizable and surprising. Perfect for the adventurous gin drinker who wants to branch out from the typical London Dry. However, if a traditional unflavoured gin is your preference, serve the McQueen Highland Dry over ice, with an aromatic soda water and garnished with juniper berries, rosemary and pink peppercorns.

McQueen's gins are also great for cocktail experiments, with their strong and varied flavours. Their strength of character means they're also excellent sipping gins.

Propelled by a flurry of awards, Dale and Vicky expanded. In 2019 they launched their new distillery (opposite, top). They also recently redesigned their bottle with a fresh design.

The distillery is at Callander, at the gateway of the famous Loch Lomond, in the Trossachs National Park.

Gin Bothy Distillery and Gin

Glamis, Angus
Distillery, tasting rooms and shop

ESSENTIAL INFORMATION

Key botanicals (Gin Bothy Original):
   juniper, rosemary, heather, hawthorn
   root, milk thistle, Scots pine needle

Output: 3,000 bottles a year

Location: Kirk Wynd, Forfar, DD8 1RT

Telephone: 01575 570111

Email: info@ginbothy.co.uk

Website: www.ginbothy.co.uk

Facebook: www.facebook.com/theginbothy

Instagram: @theginbothy

Twitter: @TheGinBothy

Opening hours:

Gin Bothy Experience and tastings
   Thursday-Sunday 1100-1700

Special tastings available monthly

Book via website

Other reasons to go: St Fergus's Well, Ark
Hill, Meffan Institute

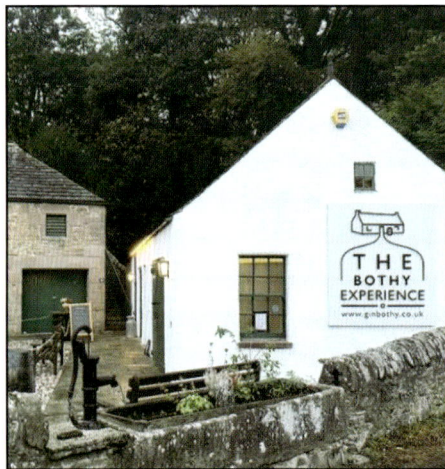

Kim Cameron founded Gin Bothy (bottom left) on an ideal: making the most of what the land has to offer. Its location in the foothills of the Angus Glens is ideal for this endeavour, ideal for Kim and her team of foragers to find local botanicals such as pine needles, heather, milk thistle and hawthorn for use in their signature spirit, Gin Bothy Original. The resulting taste, smell and feel reflects the freshness of Scottish woodland.

Kim started her gin journey (under her mum's instructions) by infusing the leftover berry juice from her homemade and award-winning jam with a gin she bought in from another distillery. She soon became frustrated that she had no control over the final product, so she decided to make her own.

Kim recommends serving Gin Bothy Original with ice, tonic and a slice of fresh orange to bring out the citrus in the gin, or rosemary to enhance its herby features. As a cocktail pour, try mixing Bothy Original with thyme syrup, freshly squeezed lime juice, a dash of celery bitters and a sprig of rosemary to make a refreshing summer cocktail.

She also has a gin for winter: Gin Bothy Gunshot (opposite, middle) which is great as a sipping gin, or mixed with ginger ale or warm apple juice and an orange stuffed with cloves to make a terrific gin-based alternative to mulled wine.

And not forgetting her origins, Kim also produces fruit-infused gins which come in a variety of flavours – strawberry, raspberry, blueberry, rhubarb and sloe. The gin might taste even better when you know that if you return an empty bottle to Bothy, you get a discount on your next purchase.

Gin Bothy is located outside Kirriemuir, known as the 'little red town', a reference

to the reddish sandstone from which the town's older properties are built. Its history dates back to the earliest recorded times when it appears to have been a major ecclesiastical centre, and later had a reputation for witchcraft. Some older houses still feature a 'witches stane' to ward off evil. The playwright J. M. Barrie, who created Peter Pan, was born and buried here and a statue of the boy who never grew up stands in the town square.

As we went to press, the Gin Bothy Experience in the nearby village of Glamis was open Thursday to Sunday from 11 am to 5 pm. At the Bothy Experience, you can learn about the founding of Gin Bothy. Tastings can be booked via email or their website, where you can also view their cultural events calendar.

They also produce cider, jam, syrups and chutney, which are available to buy in their Bothy Larder shop (top right) in Glamis.

Bothy? A Scottish term for a hut, a small cottage or a temporary shelter. Kim sees her distillery both as a refuge and the embodiment of Scottish heritage.

Arbikie Distillery

Inverkeilor, Angus
Distillery, shop, bar and café

ESSENTIAL INFORMATION

Key botanicals (Nàdar Gin): juniper, lemon
grass, makrut lime
(Kirsty's Gin): juniper, blaeberry, carline
thistle, kelp
Output: not disclosed
Location: Arbikie Highland Estate,
Inverkeilor, Arbroath, DD11 4UZ
Telephone: 01241 830770
Email: info@arbikie.com
Website: www.arbikie.com
Facebook: www.facebook.com/arbikie
Instagram: @arbikiedistillery
Twitter: @Arbikie

Opening hours:
Wednesday-Sunday 1000-1730

Other reasons to go: Lunan Bay, Murton
Farm, train journey to V&A Dundee

Brothers Iain, John and David Stirling founded Arbikie Distillery on their family estate in 2014. Over a few drinks in New York, the brothers had a *eureka* moment: they realized that all the ingredients needed for high-quality spirits were growing on the farm. With a disused dairy shed waiting to be converted, they knew that the idea had legs. The estate, on the east coast of Scotland close to Montrose, has been in the Stirling family for four generations. Arbikie claims to be Scotland's first farm-to-bottle distillery. Spirits are made from scratch on site and evoke their unique environment. They use their own juniper and botanicals grown on site, as well as their own water. The mission? To set new standards in the industry and be a climate-positive distillery, using solar energy, recycling primary waste products and employing sustainable farming practices.

The first spirits were ready at the end of 2014, and Kirsty's Gin (opposite, top right, middle bottle) went on sale in the summer of 2015. Named after its creator, Master Distiller Kirsty Black, it is made using the one-shot method with their own base spirit, (made from potatoes from the farm) with kelp, blaeberries and carline thistle as botanicals to capture the elements of sea, rock and land that characterise the distillery's coastal location. Kirsty recommends serving the gin with a quality tonic, a handful of blueberries and a lemon twist, or in a Gimlet.

AK's Gin (opposite, top right, right-hand bottle) was launched to celebrate Burns Night in 2017, and was named after the Stirling siblings' late father Alexander Kirkwood Stirling. The gin is distilled from

farm-grown wheat, flavoured with black pepper, mace and cardamom for an earthy, spicy taste, and honey from Arbikie's beehives to add buttery smoothness. Arbikie recommends serving this with ice, ginger beer and a lime or orange wedge.

The groundbreaking Nàdar Gin (previous page) is their most recent addition to the range. Named after the Gaelic for 'nature', Nàdar is among the first climate-positive gins – so you can drink it with a clear conscience in the knowledge that you're saving 1.53kg of carbon emissions. It took five years of research by Kirsty Black with the James Hutton Institute in Dundee to develop the gin and prove its environmental credentials. The gin is distilled from farm-grown peas which need no nitrogen fertiliser, thereby avoiding its environmental impact. The peas also benefit the ecosystem by supporting pollenating insects and improving soil quality.

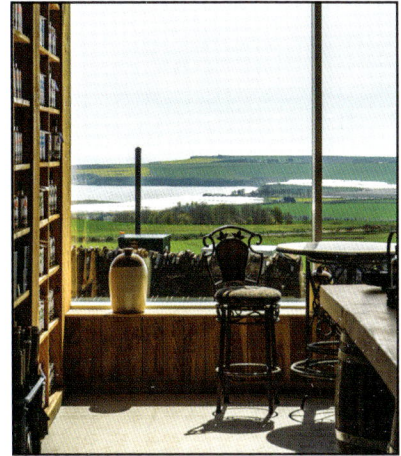

As well as being revolutionary, Nàdar Gin tastes terrific. It is silky smooth and the refreshing lemongrass and makrut lime are complemented by more classical botanicals. It is best served with a quality tonic and a slice of fresh ginger for a spicy accompaniment to the lemongrass.

The range can be bought from the online shop and the farm. Visitors can come and enjoy lunch or drinks at the café and bar with stunning views over the fields of Arbikie and down to Lunan Bay. Book a distillery tour via their website to learn how the gin is distilled from scratch using their range of homegrown crops.

Lussa Gin

Ardlussa, Isle of Jura
Distillery

ESSENTIAL INFORMATION

Key botanicals (Lussa Gin): juniper, coriander seed, lemon balm leaf, lemon thyme, elderflower, rosehip, rose petals, limeflower, honeysuckle, Scots pine, bog-myrtle, ground elder leaf, sea lettuce, water mint

Output: 10,000 bottles a year

Location: The Stables, Ardlussa, PA60 7XW

Telephone: 01496 820196

Email: contact@lussagin.com

Website: www.lussagin.com

Facebook: www.facebook.com/lussagin

Instagram: @lussagin

Twitter: @LussaGin

Opening hours:
Monday-Friday 1000-1630

Other reasons to go: Gulf of Corryvreckan, Paps of Jura, Lussa Gin Ardlussa, Isle of Jura Distillery

Ella Carr writes: The Isle of Jura, off Scotland's west coast, really is remote. Overshadowed by its mountain range, The Paps of Jura, it has a human population of 230, outnumbered by 6,000 red deer. Just 20 people live in and around Ardlussa on the northern coast, where Lussa Gin (bottom left) is made, reached via a 25-mile single track from Jura's ferry port. It's no wonder that George Orwell, who wrote *1984* on Jura's northern tip, called it the most 'un-get-at-able' place in the world.

Lussa's founders Alicia, Claire and Georgina (opposite, bottom) were seduced by its pristine beauty and isolation. Their gin is as much a reflection of the resilience needed to live on the island as it is of Jura's unique natural setting. All 15 of Lussa's botanicals are painstakingly foraged from nearby glens, lochs, bogs and seas: the unique setting makes for a unique botanical profile, among them bog-myrtle, sea lettuce, ground elder and Scots pine.

The botanicals are distilled in Hamish, their traditional 200-litre Portuguese hand-crafted copper still. Leaves, needles, cones and roots are added to the pot along with the neutral spirit and spring water from the Ardlussa hills, while the flowers and petals are suspended in a column above the pot, giving their flavour and aroma to the vapour as it passes. The mix is then warmed using a *bain-marie*, and the spirit is gently distilled over the course of a day.

Unusually for a British gin, even the orris root and juniper berries are locally grown. Juniper has grown in Scotland since the last ice age, but is currently under threat from disease. Jura's remoteness has spared the juniper somewhat, and the girls are trying to help it along by planting 500 bushes

around Lussa Glen. As we went to press, their harvest would have been ready.

The distillery is open Monday to Friday from 10 am until 4.30 pm for anyone adventurous enough to make the journey; but there's plenty on Jura to make the journey worthwhile. Aside from the thrill of visiting one of Scotland's (perhaps even Europe's) last true wildernesses, the island is also scattered with relics from its Stone Age and Mesolithic past, and host to a dizzying array of wildlife – including golden eagles, sea eagles, hen harries, owls, adders, grey seals, dolphins and porpoises.

Badachro Gin and Distillery

Badachro, Gairloch
Distillery

Looking for gin that is authentically small batch, a product of its environment, pure and individual? Badachro ticks all the boxes. The batches are a maximum of 180 bottles, and diluted with rain and loch water from the stunning Scottish highland landscape surrounding the distillery.

Gordon and Vanessa (opposite, middle right) met in the Badachro Inn and married after just twelve weeks. Twenty-six years later the duo and their family are well established features in the local community.

Their previous careers in hospitality and advertising fitted them for their new life. They had moved back to Badachro, a tiny hamlet in the far northwest near Gairloch, in order to opt out of the rat race, starting a bed and breakfast.

They didn't set out to make gin – but noticing their guests' keen interest in taking away a product that would remind them of the area, Vanessa suggested room scents. Gordon's reply was 'why not a liqueur?'

Badachro Gin (left), their core product, is a classic London Dry but with unexpected complexity and depth, leading not just with juniper but myrtle. Gordon says that this reflects its surroundings (opposite, bottom) because on the face of it the local way of life is simple, yet Gairloch's dramatic wilderness, mountains and seascape scenery strikes unexpectedly deep chords.

Badachro Gairloch Coastal Gin is very different: bright and fresh, with fennel and wild thyme dominating, along with two seaweeds. Their third gin, Storm Strength, is 57%. They have now added Dancing Puffin Vodka and a classic single malt whisky to their range. Badachro is increasingly on the map for visitors, and a distillery visit is the making of a trip to this remote area.

Kintyre Gin and Beinn an Tuirc Distillery

Campbeltown, Kintyre
Distillery

ESSENTIAL INFORMATION
Key botanicals (Kintyre Botanical Gin):
   juniper, coriander, liquorice, almond,
   cassia, cubeb berries, orange, lemon,
   Icelandic moss, sheep sorrel
Output: 20,000 bottles a year
Location: Torrisdale Castle Estate,
   Carradale, near Campbeltown, Kintyre
Telephone: 01583 431528
Email: info@kintyregin.com
Website: www.kintyregin.com
Facebook: www.facebook.com/kintyregin/
Instagram: @kintyredistillery
Twitter: @kintyredistil

Opening hours:
Monday-Sunday 1100-1600

Other reasons to go: Woodland walks,
private beach, holiday accomodation

Beinn an Tuirc Distillers was formed in 2016 and began production in July 2017. The company's initial goal was to make Kintyre Botanical Gin, a locally hand-crafted, sustainably distilled product.

From the outset they aimed to keep sustainability at the heart of the business The gin still is powered by their own hydroelectricity, keeping carbon emissions low. They source their water from the eponymous hill, 'Beinn an Tuirc' which translates from Gaelic as 'The Hill of the Wild Boar'. It is the highest point in Kintyre, located right above the distillery building (below). The distillery also has a dedicated tree plantation nearby, where oak trees are planted to offset any carbon used in the distillation processes and distribution.

The first bottle of Kintyre Gin was released in 2017, and since then Beinn an Tuirc have added several more craft spirits to the range and opened a distillery shop, tasting room, cafe and gin school. They want to encourage visitors to this remote and little-known part of Scotland, benefitting both themselves and other local businesses.

Sea Glass Gin and Deerness Distillery

Deerness, Orkney

Distillery

ESSENTIAL INFORMATION

Key botanicals (Sea Glass Gin): juniper, orange peel, lemon verbena, cucumber, lavender, mint, tarragon,
Output: 20,000 bottles a year
Location: Newhall, KW17 2QJ
Telephone: 01856 741264
Email: info@deernessdistillery.com
Website: www.deernessdistillery.com
Facebook: www.facebook.com/DeernessDistillery
Instagram: @deerness_distillery
Twitter: @deer_distillery

Opening hours:
Monday-Friday 1000-1700

Other reasons to go: Skara Brae Prehistoric Village, Ring of Brodgar, Maeshowe, Scapa Flow

Probably the most remote distillery in the guide: the Orkney Island group off the NE tip of Scotland is two hours by ferry from Scrabster on mainland Scotland – out on a limb by any measure. You dock at Stromness on Mainland Orkney and from there you must cross the island via the main town, Kirkwall, then head out over a narrow neck of land to East Mainland Orkney where you eventually reach the rugged, windswept coastal area known as Deerness. Here, there is not much except ancient legends and Deerness Distillery.

Perhaps unexpectedly, it's a lovely place to visit. Adelle and Stuart Brown's operation offers a visitor experience with tours of the whole distillery area, tastings and a well-stocked shop displaying not only the distillery's gin and vodka – plus a unique collection of tonic waters from across the UK and Europe – but also unique Orkney Islands products such as locally-crafted glass and thoughtfully selected Scottish homeware and crafts.

Sea Glass Gin (left), their multi-award winning Orkney gin, was released in Spring 2017 as the result of much experimentation. Sea Glass Gin takes you on a pleasurable sensory experience through warm spices, bold citrus and juniper. It is a reflection of the Orkney Islands' ever-changing seascape, which is also captured in their bottle label.

Pair it with an Indian tonic water or elderflower-infused tonic. Adelle and Stuart recommend Franklin & Sons Pineapple Mixer with Almond. Garnish with any fruits you have handy in your fridge: blueberries, lemon or kiwi all go especially well with this versatile spirit.

Thompson Bros. Mediterranean Organic Gin and Dornoch Distillery

Dornoch, Sutherland
Distillery and shop

ESSENTIAL INFORMATION

Key botanicals (Thompson Bros. Mediterranean Organic Gin): juniper, coriander seed, cardamom, black pepper, dried lime, dried lemon, fresh lemon peel, orange peel, meadowsweet, bay leaf, bergamot, thyme, rosemary

Output: 3,000 bottles a year

Location: Unit 3C, Station Square, Dornoch, IV25 3PB

Telephone: 01862 810637

Email: info@dornochdistillery.com

Website: www..thompsonbrosdistillers.com

Facebook: www.facebook.com/dornochdistillery

Instagram: @dornochdistillery

Opening hours: check shop opening times on their website

Other reasons to go: Dornoch Castle Hotel Whisky Bar

Dornoch Distillery was launched in 2016 by brothers Phil and Simon Thompson. Not content with creating a renowned and successful whisky bar in their home town of Dornoch, the business-savvy brothers organized a successful crowdfund to finance the distillery.

Based in a renovated Victorian Fire Station on the site of Dornoch Castle Hotel, Phil and Simon transformed their passion for distilling into a business producing craft whisky and gin.

Following the success of the initial launch in 2016, Dornoch released its signature Thompson Bros. Organic Highland Gin a year later in 2017. The distillery also produces a range of limited-edition craft whiskies.

Breaking away from their experimental Highland Gin, Dornoch introduced their Mediterranean Organic Gin in November 2021. Inspired by typical Mediterranean flavours, it is crafted from blend of seasonal botanicals including bergamot, lemon peel, orange peel, rosemary, thyme and bay leaf.

Their unique distilling process is carefully thought out. The gin is non-chill filtered to maintain flavour and texture. Individual infusions of the citrus and herbs are slowly blended with the base botanical blend, which is then diluted over a period of two weeks.

Their careful crafting of Mediterranean Organic Gin (left and opposite) has been widely acclaimed, the gin achieved a gold medal at the World Gin Awards in the Contemporary Scottish Gin category. It is best served simply over ice with tonic and a twist of lemon.

In keeping with the distillery's whisky roots, the Mediterranean Gin comes in

traditional whisky bottle shape, and has a light and contemporary label designed by luxury fashion designer and fellow Scot, Karen Mabon.

Visitors are welcomed to Dornoch Castle Hotel, where they can enjoy a wide range of craft whiskies, or of course the Mediterranean Gin served in the bar where the idea for Dornoch Distillery was born.

Rock Rose Gin and Dunnet Bay Distillers

Dunnet, Caithness
Distillery, shop and tours

ESSENTIAL INFORMATION

Key botanicals (Rock Rose Gin): juniper, liquorice, cinnamon, water mint, blaeberry, hawthorn berry, rowan berry, *Rhodiola rosea*, sea buckthorn

Output: 105,000 bottles a year

Location: Dunnet Bay Distillery, Thurso, KW14 8XD

Telephone: 01847 851287

Email: info@rockrosegin.co.uk

Website: www.dunnetbaydistillers.co.uk

Facebook: www.facebook.com/rockrosegin

Instagram: @rockrosegin

Twitter: @rockrosegin

Opening hours:
Monday-Saturday 1000-1700
Closes 1600 in winter
(advanced booking advised)

Other reasons to go: Surf lessons with Northcoast Watersports, Maryanns Cottage, Castle of Mey, Dunnet Beach, Dunnet forest wood carvings, Northern Sands Hotel

The Rock Rose journey can be traced back as far as the distillers' university days, where Claire and Martin (opposite, top right) spoke of one day setting up their own business together in their home of Caithness. With qualifications in chemical and process engineering, Martin decided to pursue a career running a process plant offshore in the oil and gas industry. Claire, with her skills in hospitality and tourism, went to work in the tourism industry.

The duo were always interested in running their own distillery but were unable to afford a distilling licence. Once the battle with HMRC over licensing had been won, they immediately moved from France back home to Caithness to buy their first still.

They built their own house and distillery, and opened the door in 2014. Once the first copper pot still – nicknamed Elizabeth – was installed, they perfected the recipe for Rock Rose Gin. They made and sold 9,000 bottles in the first quarter of distilling and the first batch sold out by pre-orders within forty-eight hours of release in August 2014.

Claire and Martin's previous careers helped them enormously with the business. Martin was used to installing and operating heavy machinery, and Claire's background enabled her to manage and develop the customer focused side – marketing, retail, hospitality, tours and events. Their aim to be self-employed in their home of Caithness was realised.

Each bottle is hand-filled, individually wax-sealed, batch-numbered and hand-signed before leaving the distillery. They expanded the range with Citrus Coastal, Pink Grapefruit Old Tom, Smoked Orange, and Navy Strength, and release seasonal editions of the gin four times a year.

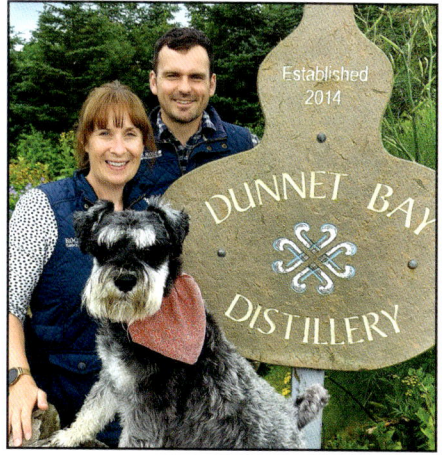

Now they employ 14 people, and their gin is distributed and enjoyed in over 20 countries. Rock Rose Gin was chosen by CoolBrands in 2021 and 2022 and won numerous awards including Scottish Gin Distillery of the Year 2019, and Great Taste Awards, Navy Strength Gin and Holy Grass Vodka (right). Their newest Smoked Orange Edition features smoky lapsang souchong tea and zesty organic orange peel. They suggest you garnish Rock Rose Original Edition with toasted rosemary and a curl of orange peel.

Isle of Tiree Distillery

Hynish, Isle of Tiree
Distillery

ESSENTIAL INFORMATION
Key botanicals (Tyree Gin): juniper, ladies bedstraw, kelp, water mint
(Hebridean Pink Gin): juniper, cinnamon, sweet peels, raspberries, black pepper
Output: not disclosed
Location: 1A West Hynish, Isle of Tiree, PA77 6UF
Telephone: 07591 005871
Email: ian@tireewhiskycompany.com
Website: www.tyreegin.com
Facebook: www.facebook.com/tireedistillery
Instagram: @tireedistillery
Twitter: @TyreeGin

Opening hours:
Monday-Saturday 1100-1700

Other reasons to go: Skerryvore Lighthouse, The Ringing Stone, Hynish Heritage Trail

Tyree was the old spelling of this island's name. The modern spelling of Tiree first appeared on a map produced by John Cowley in 1734. The island – also known as *Tìr an Eòrna* (Land of Barley) in Gaelic – was once home to 50 distillers, but, unlike other islands, never got a modern a distillery until recently. Tiree Whisky Company Ltd was formed to preserve and promote the island's whisky heritage and revive its distilling history, and The Isle of Tiree Distillery is the island's first legal operational distillery since the 19thC. As well as being one of one of the smallest, most traditional producers of whisky in Scotland, the distillery makes the award-winning Tyree Gin and Hebridean Pink Gin.

Tyree Gin (left, top) reflects the landscape where it is distilled. The kelp harvested from icy waters provides sweetness and a salty, seaside taste. Floral, grassy and vanilla flavours come from botanicals collected from the inland machair ground and combine with juniper, water mint and angelica to create a fresh, pure island spirit. In 2022, it was awarded Gold at the Spirits Business Gin Masters and Bronze at the International Wine and Spirits Competition.

Hebridean Pink Gin (left, bottom) is distilled using seven botanicals including juniper, raspberries, sweetpeels, cinnamon and black pepper. Once distilled, natural raspberry concentrate is added, resulting in a fresh contemporary gin with a sweet caramel aroma. As well as numerous past awards, in 2022 Hebridean Pink Gin was awarded Silver at the Spirits Business Gin Masters and Bronze in the International Wine and Spirits Competition.

Pixel Spirits Distillery, Gin School and Old Ferry Bar

North Ballachulish, Fort William
Distillery, bar and gin school

ESSENTIAL INFORMATION

Key botanicals (Devil's Staircase Highland Spiced Gin): juniper, coriander, cardamom, cassia bark, nutmeg, orange peel, lemon peel, grains of paradise **(Drookit Piper Highland Citrus Gin):** juniper, coriander, pomelo peel, lime peel, lemon peel, orange peel, kaffir lime leaves **(Drookit Hoose Highland Dry Gin):** juniper, coriander, rowan berries, heather, silver birch sap, rosehips, grapefruit peel

Output: 12,000 bottles a year

Location: Old Ferry Road, Loch Leven Hotel, North Ballachulish, PH33 6SA

Telephone: 07443 656528

Email: info@pixelspiritsltd.co.uk

Website: www.pixelspiritsltd.co.uk

Facebook: www.facebook.com/ pixelspirits

Instagram: @pixel_spirits

Twitter: @pixelspirits

Opening hours:

Old Ferry Bar
  Every day 1230-2300

Experiences/tours by appointment only

Other reasons to go: Loch Leven, Glencoe, West Highland Way

In 2015, husband and wife team Craig and Noru Innes decided to convert a dilapidated 17thC barn in the grounds of the Loch Leven Hotel into a craft gin distillery. After two years of building work and with the help of family and friends, in 2017 Pixel Spirits Distillery and Gin School opened its doors and launched their first product – Devil's Staircase Highland Spiced Gin. This smooth, warming gin takes its name from the most treacherous part of the West Highland Way, minutes from the distillery's doorstep, and has won numerous international awards.

To make their gin, juniper and coriander are steeped in neutral grain spirit overnight. The rest of the botanicals are added just before distillation. Their 100-litre stainless steel still, called Orsetta ('little bear'), makes batches of 75 bottles at a time. They also have a larger, 500-litre still named The Big Yin ('the big one') after Scottish comedian, Billy Connelly. Where possible, the fruit used in all their gins is hand-peeled and dehydrated in-house to ensure premium taste and quality.

Also in the hotel's grounds is The Old Ferry Bar, dating from the 1800s. It stocks more than 50 gins, including the Devil's Staircase and other home-distilled tipples such as Drookit Piper Highland Citrus and Highland Dry. The bar's artisan range also includes exciting products like a Chanterelle Gin – made with mushrooms suspended in a pot still above liquid level, allowing a gentle vapour infusion and savoury flavour.

Pixel offers gin classes in the former cowshed of the distillery. For £69-£99pp, you'll learn about key botanicals and create your own recipe on a mini still. The class lasts four hours and can cater for groups of two to eight – group discounts are available on request. Email them for dates and availability.

183

Shetland Reel Gin and The Shetland Distillery Company

Unst, Shetland Islands
Distillery

ESSENTIAL INFORMATION

Key botanicals (Shetland Reel Gin):
   juniper, coriander seed, cinnamon, citrus
   peel, apple mint, bladderwrack seaweed

Output: 67,000 bottles a year

Location: Saxa Vord Distillery, Haroldswick,
   ZE2 9EF

Telephone: 01957 711217

Email: info@shetlandreel.com

Website: www.shetlandreel.com

Facebook: www.facebook.com/
   shetlandreel

Instagram: @shetlandreel

Twitter: @shetlandreelgin

Opening hours:
Guided tastings held year-round Monday-
   Saturday from 1200, bookings only

Other reasons to go: Unst Boat Haven, Unst
Heritage Centre

The Shetland Islands are at the very northern tip of the British Isles, where the North Sea meets the Atlantic Ocean, and Unst – where Saxa Vord distillery is located – is their most northerly point. Closer, in fact, to Norway in both distance and culture than it is to Scotland. Far-flung places such as these – whose regional identities are unique – have a knack for producing excellent craft gins.

Shetland Reel Gin (opposite, top, left-hand bottle) – which started out as a small batch operation only available on Shetland – has steadily grown in reputation, and is now stocked globally. They've stayed true to the small craft ethos however, producing all gin on site and taste-testing each batch.

The distillery was founded by two couples, united by their ambition to set up the most northerly gin and whisky distillery in Britain. Frank and Debbie Strang had already developed Saxa Vord (formerly an RAF base) into an award-winning tourist resort. Stuart and Wilma Nickerson were founders of The Malt Whisky Company. September 2014 was the couples' first commercial distillation run to make Shetland Reel Gin, with all 55 of these limited edition bottles presented in Shetland tweed bags.

The aim was to make a traditional gin with a Shetland twist: the modest botanical count of eight includes classics such as coriander seeds, cinnamon and citrus peel, plus the unique ingredient of Unst-harvested apple mint – a member of the mint family with a slightly fruitier aroma, that gives the gin a subtle and refreshing minty finish.

Shetland Reel Ocean Sent Gin evokes the sea through the addition of Bladderwrack, a type of local seaweed (above, right-hand bottle). Our personal favourite, Shetland Reel Simmer Gin (above, middle bottle), is inspired by the Shetland's crepuscular summer skies – when the days seem endless and the sun barely falls below the horizon, known to Shetlanders as Simmer Dim.

They also produce Countdown Gin (previous page), inspired by SaxaVord Spaceport. As we went to press, Unst was counting down to Shetland's first satellite launch. Also in the range is Shetland Reel Filska Gin (middle) made with red grapefruit; and a Rhubarb and Bramble Gin Liqueur (bottom).

Each January they produce a new cask-aged gin, as a nod to Shetland's seafaring history. It celebrates the annual fire festival, Up Helly Aa, held in Lerwick on the last Tuesday of January, which sees more than a thousand Shetlanders dressed as Vikings in procession through the streets with flaming torches and setting fire to a longship.

Kinrara Distillery

Aviemore, Cairngorms
Distillery and shop

ESSENTIAL INFORMATION
Key botanicals (Kinrara Highland Dry):
  juniper, coriander, liquorice, cardamom,
  rosehips, orange peel, lemon peel,
  rowanberries
Output: not disclosed
Location: Lynwilg Farm Steading, Aviemore,
  PH22 1PZ
Telephone: 01479 816362
Email: info@kinraradistillery.com
Website: www.kinraradistillery.com
Facebook: www.facebook.com/
  KinraraDistillery
Instagram: @kinraradistillery

Opening hours:
Monday-Sunday 1000-1700

Other reasons to go: Cairngorms National
Park, Craigellachie National Nature
Reserve, Rothiemurchus

Kinrara Distillery, born in 2017, is set in the magnificent rolling landscape of the Cairngorms, outside Aviemore, on the Kinrara Estate, from which the distillery takes its name. The area is outstandingly beautiful as well as historically interesting, certainly worth a visit.

The team have been inspired by the beauty of the landscape and the stories associated with it. Formerly a milking shed, their re-purposed distillery is designed with the rich history of the area in mind.

Kinrara's multi award-winning craft gins are made in small batches blending traditional spirit production methods with contemporary taste – from thoughtful ingredient selection to bold experimentation to the bottling process. The distillery successfully established itself on the Scottish gin scene because of its solid relationships with wholesalers and customers and its reputation for hard work.

Kinrara's Highland Dry Gin was awarded Best Scottish Contemporary at the 2021 and 2022 World Gin Awards. Another product, Ginny, is part of their Artist Edition collection, and picked up the London Dry Gin of the Year at the 2021 Scottish Gin Awards. Ginny is joined by Struan and Freya to complete the collection, with the bottles designed by young Dundee artist, Kat Baxter.

Kinrara currently produces 12 gins. Paying a visit is a must if you are in north-east Scotland: the daily tastings take place against a backdrop of unforgettable Highland scenery. Left, one of the Artist Collection gins; next page, top left, their well-presented shop.

Avva Scottish Gin and Moray Distillery Ltd

Elgin, Speyside
Distillery

ESSENTIAL INFORMATION

Key botanicals (Avva Scottish Gin):
juniper, coriander, lemon, sweet orange,
mint, nettle, dandelion, rowan, red clover
Output: 8,000 bottles a year
Location: 10 Chanonry Road North, IV30 6NB
Telephone: 01343 548700
Email: info@avvascottishgin.co.uk
Website: www.moraydistilleryltd.co.uk/
Facebook: www.facebook.com/
avvascottishgin
Instagram: @avvascottishgin
Twitter: @AvvaScottishGin

Opening hours:
Tours held in May, and by pre-booking with
six weeks' notice through selected tour
operators between May and September

Other reasons to go: Elgin Cathedral,
Spynie Palace, Moray Motor Museum,
Duffus Castle

Moray is Scotland's historic home of distilling, containing Speyside, where many of the world's most famous single malt whisky brands are produced. Gin is the newcomer, with small distilleries springing up rapidly. Single malt whisky tours are a key draw for visitors and as part of the Spirit of Speyside Whisky Festival, Moray Distillery Ltd hosts open days, where visitors get a behind-the-scenes experience, plus a tasting of their signature product, Avva Scottish Gin.

Jill Brown's is a genuine small batch operation, launched in 2016, making 220 bottles of Avva Gin from the heart of each run. She produces from what can claim to be the UK's first Scottish made gin still named 'JJ' after Jill's two grandmothers, Jessie and Jean. The aroma is juniper led, followed by herbaceous, floral and citrus elements. On the tongue it's smooth juniper combined with balanced herbaceous flavours and the finish is fresh citrus and mint. Besides Avva, Jill produces a navy strength gin, a cask-matured gin and some liqueurs.

After one sip of Avva you naturally want to Avvanother, but the name is far from being a droll joke. In Dravidian, one of the ancient languages of India, *avva* is a respected mother, grandmother or older woman; and in Hebrew the same word means ruin. So the name deftly nods not just to Jill's grandmothers, but to gin's old reputation as Mother's Ruin.

Visiting the Elgin area is also great for Elgin's cathedral, which features on Avva Gin's label. The cathedral opened in 1224 and is known as the Lantern of the North because it shines out as one of Scotland's most impressive and numinous buildings.

Gordon Castle Gin

Fochabers, Morayshire
Distillery

ESSENTIAL INFORMATION

Key botanicals (Gordon Castle Gin):
juniper, coriander seed, liquorice,
cinnamon, cassia bark, lemon peel,
orange peel, nutmeg, mint, lavender
Output: 10,000 bottles a year
Location: Gordon Castle Walled Garden,
Fochabers, IV32 7PQ
Telephone: 01343 612312
Email: info@gordoncastlescotland.com
Website: www.gordoncastlescotland.com
Facebook: www.facebook.com/
GordonCastleScotland
Instagram: @gordancastlescotland
Twitter: @gordoncastlegin

Opening hours:
The Walled Garden Cafe & Shop
Wednesday-Sunday 1100-1600
The Walled Garden
Every day 1000-1600

**Other reasons to go: Moray Monster
Trails, Fochabers Folk Museum & Heritage
Centre, Loch Oire**

The history of Gordon Castle Gin dates back to the late 18thC when the castle (after which the gin is named) was enlarged by the fourth Duke of Gordon to become one of Scotland's most palatial houses. Located in Speyside, Gordon Castle has links with the spirits industry and in 1823 the Duke put legislation through Parliament which first legalized whisky distilling. The castle was used as an auxiliary hospital for soldiers wounded in the First World War and a barracks in the Second. When it was sold in the 1930s to pay punitive death duties after the war, it fell into disrepair until rescued by Lieutenant General Sir George Gordon Lennox, a descendant of the fourth Duke of Gordon. In 2008 his grandson, Angus, and his wife Zara took over the running of the estate and transformed it into a visitor attraction offering accommodation, self-catering holiday cottages and salmon fishing. In 2014, they launched their craft gin, Gordon Castle (bottom middle); a luxury beauty and bath range; and a collection of tweed and bone china products.

Gordon Castle Gin is made from botanicals picked in the estate's Scottish Walled Garden by head gardener Ed (next page, bottom left). Try serving 50 ml of Gordon Castle Gin with lemon, lime, fresh mint and a premium tonic with plenty of ice.

You could also try Gordon Castle Raspberry Gin Liqueur (left-hand bottle, and next page, middle left) and Gordon Castle Plum Gin Liqueur (right-hand bottle). All the gins can be bought from the online shop, or in the cafe.

Prices start at £5.99 for a Gordon Castle 5 cl miniature bottle. The Gordon Castle Gin Trio Set is available at just £17.95,

reaching £47.95 for their best seller, which is a personalised, engraved bottle of Gordon Castle Botanical Gin. Their Engraved Gin Lovers Hamper is a also perfect gift. This includes a 50-cl bottle of Gordon Castle Plum and Raspberry Gin Liqueurs, LED cork lights and a 70-cl engraved bottle of Gordon Castle Botanical Gin packaged in a luxury hamper.

House of Elrick Gin

Newmachar, Aberdeenshire
Distillery

ESSENTIAL INFORMATION

Key botanicals (House of Elrick Gin):
juniper, coriander seed, citrus peel, pink peppercorn, sweet fennel, heather, rose petal

Output: 26,000 bottles a year

Location: Elrick House, AB21 7PY

Telephone: 01651 862141

Email: info@houseofelrick.com

Website: www.houseofelrick.co.uk

Facebook: www.facebook.com/houseofelrick

Instagram: @houseofelrick

Twitter: @HouseOfElrick

Opening hours:
Visits by appointment only

Other reasons to go: Pitmedden Garden, Kirkhill Forest, Dyce stones, Museum of Farming Life

Fans of the TV show *Dragon's Den* might remember Stuart Ingram, (next page, top left) who appeared on the show in 2018 with his House of Elrick Gin (bottom left). Stuart won an £80,000 investment deal but later turned it down as he and Peter Jones couldn't agree on a percentage stake for the whole company. However, this hasn't hindered the success of House of Elrick Gin – quite the contrary. Since the show in 2018, Stuart has managed to completely regenerate the Elrick Estate, which includes a ten-bedroom 18thC listed house, a walled garden with an apple store, and a gin distillery.

It is located in the lowlands of Aberdeenshire and produces a wide range of spirits including its Signature Original Gin, a selection of rums and a range of pre-mixed cans. One of the key botanicals, rose petals, adds more than just flavour to the gin – it is also historically interesting. Bonnie Prince Charlie visited House of Elrick and gave it the Jacobite rose that still grows in its gardens. The purpose-built artisan distillery houses a 500-litre bespoke copper still aptly named Charlie, and produces batches of 600 bottles per run, making it genuinely small batch.

House of Elrick also produce an Old Tom Gin (next page, bottom right) made from the same botanicals as the Original Gin but sweetened with syrup. The range also includes a Coconut Gin, which uses the Old Tom Gin infused with a natural coconut flavour. At the beginning of 2020, they launched a range of rums, including Dark, White Mango, and Spiced Rum (next page, middle), which have now become just as popular as their gin offerings.

For the perfect serve, House of Elrick recommends adding 25 to 50 ml of their

Signature Original Gin to a deep wine glass over plenty of ice to release the botanicals' flavours. If preferred, add a light tonic for a longer drink, then add orange zest to the rim of the glass and garnish with an orange twist to intensify the tastes of rose and peppercorn.

For a refreshing summer cocktail, why not try House of Fizz: in your cocktail shaker mix 37.5 ml of Original Gin, 12.5 ml of Cointreau, 22.5 ml of fresh pineapple juice, 12.5 ml of vanilla sugar, and fill the shaker with ice. Double strain, pour into a champagne flute, top up with rose prosecco and garnish with pomegranate seeds.

All House of Elrick Spirits and pre-mixed ready-to-drink cans can be bought from House of Elrick's online shop.

Aatta Gin and Orkney Gin Company

Orkney
Distillery

ESSENTIAL INFORMATION
Key botanicals (Aatta Gin): juniper, whole
oranges, rosehip, vanilla
(Johnsmas Gin): juniper, mint, Seville
orange, rose, heather flowers
(Rhubarb Old Tom Gin): juniper, Seville
orange, cinnamon, rose petals
Output: not disclosed
Location: Burray, Orkney, KW17 2SS
Telephone: 01856 731700
Email: info@orkneygincompany.com
Website: www.orkneygincompany.com
Facebook: www.facebook.com/
orkneygincompany
Instagram: @orkneygincompany
Twitter: @OrkneyGin

Opening hours: not open to the public

Gary Watt writes: With their stunning scenery, famous history, and unique folklore tales, it would be impossible not to fall in love with the islands we call home. I come from a family of seafarers, and we love the tales of the Selkie Folk, which can be seen on our bottles. My small family team makes our spirits using local ingredients and traditional methods and enjoy telling Orkney's forgotten tales through our spirits.

We believe that you experience the essence of Orkney when you open one of our bottles. Everything you see and taste is created by hand: from picking our base botanicals, such as heather flower, crow berries, rosehip and mint on the rolling hills, to distilling the spirit slowly up to eight times for an outstanding mouthfeel, to filling and corking our beautiful bottles in our distillery overlooking Orkney's famous Scapa Flow.

Orkney Gin Company are also the makers of Scotland's first Akvavit – Orkney Akvavit (or Aquavit) – a delicious Nordic spirit which connects Orkney to its Scandinavian roots.

The distillery has, so far, produced four medal-winning gins. The latest release is Aatta (left), whose bottle won the World's Best Design in the Prestigious World Drinks Awards 2022. This is not just a good-looking bottle but an accomplished London Dry Gin which has won several taste awards including the London Spirits Competition and The Spirits Business Gin Masters.

Crofter's Tears Gin and Ice and Fire Distillery

Smerral, Latheronwheel
Distillery

ESSENTIAL INFORMATION

Key botanicals (Crofter's Tears Gin):
juniper, coriander, cardamom, cubeb, cassia, orange peel, lime peel, purple heather flowers
(Caithness Highland Gin): juniper, coriander, liquorice, orange peel, fresh lime peel, salmonberries, rhubarb
Output: not disclosed
Location: Newblack Croft, Smerral, Latheron, Caithness, KW5 6DU
Telephone: 01593 741753
Email: rookums@aol.com
Website: iceandfiredistillery.com
Facebook: www.facebook.com/ iceandfiregin
Instagram: @iceandfiregin
Twitter: @iceandfiregin

Opening hours: not open to the public

The Ice and Fire Distillery business model is all about distinguishing genuinely artisan products from mass-produced gins. They ensure their drinks are authentically handcrafted using natural ingredients, many of which they grow themselves for the freshest possible taste.

The Highland Crofter heritage of the people involved is evident in the design of the bottle, with iconic Scottish heather entwined around it and a highland stag embossed on the glass.

Many crofters in Caithness and elsewhere supplemented their income by distilling illicit whisky: there was a ready supply of water from the burns, peat from the hills and grain from the land for making moonshine. The distillers used traditional pot stills heated by naked flame. Ice and Fire have preserved this traditional method by using hand-made solid copper pot stills, and only making small batches in order to maintain the quality.

The distillery also embeds its Highland heritage into its gin recipe. Heather is the signature ingredient in Crofters Tears, best served with Fever-Tree Mediterranean tonic, a twist of lime and a bramble. Caithness Highland Gin uses rhubarb which was – and still is – a staple in any crofting garden, along with salmonberries picked from the Latheronwheel Strath. This fruity, citrus-based gin is smooth and fresh – a truly local product. Serve with tonic, a twist of lime and a raspberry.

Rademon Estate Distillery

Crossgar, Co. Down
Distillery

ESSENTIAL INFORMATION

Key botanicals (Shortcross Gin): juniper, coriander, cassia bark, orange, elderberry, green apple, elderflower, wild clover

Output: not disclosed

Location: 62 Ballynahinch Road, Downpatrick, BT30 9HS

Telephone: 02844 830001

Email: hello@shortcrossgin.com

Website: www.shortcrossgin.com

Facebook: www.facebook.com/ SHORTCROSSGIN

Instagram: @rademonestatedistillery

Opening hours:
Monday-Friday 0915-1700
Saturday 1215-1700

Other reasons to go: National Trust Rowallane Garden, Inch Abbey, Delamount Country Park, Clea Lough

David Smith writes: Rademon Estate Distillery (bottom left) is in the picturesque grounds of the Rademon Estate, around 20 miles SE of Belfast. The nearest village is Crossgar, which takes its name from *An Chrois Ghearr;* which in Gaelic means 'the short cross', and is the origin of both the name and logo of the distillery's gin, Shortcross (right).

The distillery was founded in 2012 by husband and wife team, Fiona and David Boyd-Armstrong. David had previously worked as an engineer in the defence industry and Fiona was a property surveyor.

The Rademon Estate may be familiar as a film location for productions such as *Game of Thrones.* It has its own hydroelectric dam, and fruits and flowers are grown in its hedgerows and gardens, some of which find their way into Shortcross gins.

The first gin was launched in 2014, followed in 2016 by an aged gin and a collaboration with That Boutique-y Gin Company. Shortcross currently have two gins in their core product range: Classic, and Bartender Series One.

In 2018, the distillery's visitor centre opened following a £2.5 million investment. It aims to provide guests with a comprehensive experience: they discover the world of botanicals and the process of gin and whisky distillation, and can take part in a gin and botanical tasting and a Gin & Tonic Masterclass. The distillery also hosts one-off events and activities.

Beyond gin, The Rademon Estate Distillery also produce single malt and single pot still Irish whisky.

Boatyard Gin and Distillery

Enniskillen, Co. Fermanagh
Distillery and shop

ESSENTIAL INFORMATION

Key botanicals (Boatyard Double Gin):
juniper, coriander, liquorice, grains of
paradise, unwaxed lemon peel, bog-myrtle
Output: 120,000 bottles a year
Location: 346 Lough Shore Road,
Drumcrow East, Enniskillen, BT93 7DX
Telephone: 07757 219431
Email: teresa@boatyarddistillery.com
Website: www.boatyarddistillery.com
Facebook: www.facebook.com/
theboatyarddistillery
Instagram: @boatyarddistillery
Twitter: @BoatyardDistill

Opening hours:
Monday-Saturday 0900-1700
Advanced booking required

Other reasons to go: Enniskillen Castle
Museums, Castle Cool National Trust,
Devenish Island

Sweet gale is one of the most unusual botanicals you'll come across in this guide, possibly the most unusual. It's also known as bog-myrtle, scientific name *Myrica gale*, a shrub typical of acid peat bogs, growing 1-2 m high. For centuries it's been useful to man as an insect repellant; as a remedy for stomach complaints; as a flavouring for beer; and in Denmark and Sweden for schnaps. It has a slightly sweet, resinous taste.

Joe McGirr (opposite, bottom left), founder of Boatyard Distillery (bottom left), collects it from a bog on his family's farm and uses it to flavour his Boatyard Double Gin (opposite, bottom right). Double gin? The distilling process is somewhat similar to that used in The Netherlands to make genever – the spirit is exposed to the juniper berries twice for an extra juniper blast. (A handful of other distillers in the guide use bog-myrtle, for example Ludlow on page 100.)

Joe is a wine and spirits industry professional who worked at Glenmorangie in Scotland and at Moet Hennessy before founding Boatyard. In common with a few of the most dedicated craft gin makers, he and two colleagues, Orlaith and Teresa, make their own base spirit from local grain – however, it is blended with a bought-in organic spirit before introducing the botanicals.

The result, according to The Gin Foundry's taster, is extreme when sipped neat. The grains of paradise and lemon peel whack your tongue and throat, but when mixed it becomes soft and sippable, with the complex flavours shining through. Joe's recommended garnish is a slice of grapefruit.

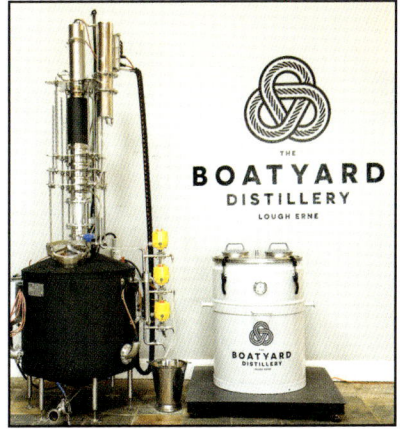

The distillery is in a lovely waterside location on Lough Erne, Northern Ireland's second biggest lake. The lough, with its many attractive islands and islets, is in fact a widened section of the River Erne and divides into two parts – Upper and Lower. The new visitor centre and renovated distillery (top left) completed 2019 are in the pleasant Tullybay neighbourhood of the Lower Lough and makes a top gin tourism experience, with tours and talks held regularly.

Boatyard makes a second gin, Old Tom (£34), aged in Pedro Ximenez barrels, sweetened with local honey. It also produces a vodka and, as the guide went to press, was planning a whisky, too.

Bertha's Revenge Gin and Ballyvolane House Spirits Co.

Castlelyons, Co. Cork
Distillery

ESSENTIAL INFORMATION

Key botanicals (Bertha's Revenge):
juniper, coriander, cardamom, cumin,
Alexander's seeds

Output: 27,000 bottles per year

Location: Castlelyons, P61 FP70

Telephone: 025 36349

Email: info@ballyvolanespirits.ie

Website: www.ballyvolanespirits.ie

Facebook: www.facebook.com/
berthasrevenge

Instagram: @ballyvolanehouse
@berthasrevenge

Twitter: @ballyvolanehouse
@berthasrevenge

Opening hours:
Tours by appointment only

Other reasons to go: Lismore Castle
Gardens and Art Gallery, Kinsale, Crawford
Gallery, English Market

Ballyvolane House – a charming country house hotel (see opposite middle, and inside back cover) – and its distillery's main product, Bertha's Revenge (bottom left), are synonymous, and sum up everything this guide loves about craft gin.

Distillers Justin Green and Antony Jackson (opposite, top left) are school friends, where they started drinking gin at 15, "possibly younger". Together they founded their distillery in 2015 and were the first to make gin using spirit distilled from whey – the clear fluid that arises when milk goes sour and the solids separate from the liquid. One or two others have copied their idea, but Bertha's Revenge remains the first of its kind and its fame is spreading.

Why use whey? First, it makes a rich, silky spirit compared to grain, that isn't dwarfed by bold botanical flavours. Second, it is produced by local cows, connecting the gin with the land. Third, it allowed them to name their gin after Bertha, Co. Kerry's most famous cow. Bertha was a local celebrity, and possibly the world's oldest cow, who died in 1993 aged 48 after giving birth to 39 calves. She was fêted even in her lifetime, once leading the local St Patrick's Day Parade. A wake was held at a local pub after she died which lasted three days, in true Irish style.

The bovine references don't stop there: in Gaelic Ballyvolane means 'place of the springing heifers'; they use water from their own well on the farm to dilute the spirit; Justin and Antony's distillery started in a (very cold) cowshed; and the whey is produced in a local cheesery.

The dominant flavour is cumin – Bertha's Revenge carries much more of the spice than other craft gins. The other botanicals

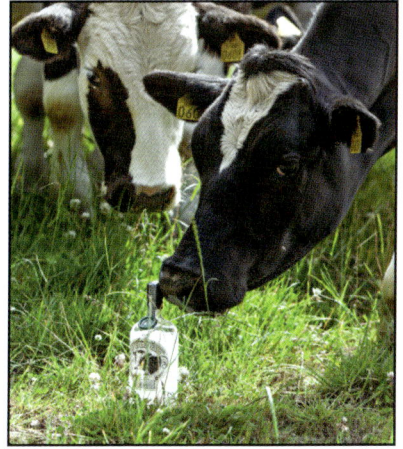

are listed opposite. The Alexander's seeds, which contribute a peppery punch, are foraged locally, of course.

Output was 500-600 bottles a week in 2018 – genuinely small batch, which with the arrival of a new still was set to triple – but keeping this admirably local enterprise firmly in the genuine microdistillery league. Production has increased significantly with the re-opening of the hospitality industry post-pandemic. Exports have grown too, with Bertha now on sale in 17 states in the USA, as well as Canada, Singapore, Japan, India, and a few European countries closer to home. Justin and Antony have introduced some new additions to the herd recently, including Bertha's Revenge Sloe Gin (below left), Bertha's Revenge Navy Strength Gin (below middle), Bertha's Revenge Crab Apple Gin Liqueur (below right), and their ready-to-drink 'Gin in a Tin' cans in the form of a B&T (Bertha and Tonic) and a Summer Cup (see back cover).

Beara Gin and Distillery

Derrymihin West, Co. Cork
Distillery

ESSENTIAL INFORMATION

Key botanicals (Beara Ocean Gin): juniper, coriander seed, cardamom, citrus peel, celery seed, fuchsia, sugar kelp seaweed, Atlantic saltwater

Output: 20,000 bottles a year

Location: Castletownbere Commercial Park, Castletownbere, P75 AX79

Telephone: 027 70861

Email: sales@thebearadistillery.ie

Website: www.thebearadistillery.ie

Facebook: www.facebook.com/ bearadistillery

Instagram: @bearadistillery

Twitter: @BearaDistillery

Opening hours: not open to the public

Inspired by the Beara peninsula and passionate about all things gin, the Power family began a journey to create their own signature gin. For 18 months they travelled across the globe, meeting distillers and gin enthusaists, and enrolling in a gin school to learn the craft of distilling and blending. Out of their wish to create a spirit which reflected the natural beauty of their home, as well as their love of the sea, Beara Ocean Gin was born. The handcrafted, small-batch gin is infused with wild Atlantic sea water and Ventry Harbour sugar kelp *saccarina latissimi*, hand-picked fuschia – the iconic flower of West Cork – and combined with traditional gin botanicals to create a well-balanced, easy drinking gin. Their pink gin (below, left) from the same range adds cranberry and rosewater to their base gin for its distinctive colour and taste.

This distillery didn't stop at gin. Their Black Cask Blend Irish Whiskey (below right, middle bottle) is a unique blend of Single Malt (below right, left-hand bottle) and Extra Char Cask Finished Single Grain Irish whiskies (below, right-hand bottle and previous page, right). Enjoy it neat with ice, or with a splash of water to open up the rich malt and toasted oak flavours. The Single Malt Irish Whiskey is similarly complex and delicious, having been aged with care in virgin new oak casks where it develops a rich colour and smooth texture. The water used to reduce the whisky is filtered spring water from the Caha mountains that separate Cork and Kerry and divide the Beara Peninsula – so you get an authentic taste of Ireland.

The Shed Distillery

Drumshanbo, Co. Leitrim
Distillery, café and shop

ESSENTIAL INFORMATION

Key botanicals (Drumshanbo Gunpowder Irish Gin): juniper, coriander seed, cardamom, lemon, grapefruit, star anise, caraway seed, kaffir lime, meadowsweet, gunpowder tea

Output: 100,000 cases a year

Location: Carrick on Shannon Road, Drumshanbo, County Leitrim

Telephone: +353 1507 9170

Email: prigney@theshedistillery.com

Website: www.thesheddistillery.com

Facebook: www.facebook.com/theshedrumshanbo.ie

Instagram: @theshedistillery

Opening hours:
Monday-Tuesday 1000-1800

Patrick Rigney had been in the drinks industry for more than 30 years when he launched the Shed Distillery in 2014, which he claims is the first distillery in Connacht for 101 years. Pat's first project was a whisky, but with a three-year ageing process, he worked on other spirits while it matured and in 2016 launched Drumshanbo Gunpowder Irish Gin (bottom left).

Gunpowder fuses traditional recipes with local ingredients such as meadowsweet, plus botanicals Pat collected on his travels. He came across gunpowder tea on a trip to Morocco, where he took part in a traditional tea ceremony. Intrigued by the pellet-shaped leaves and their slightly spicy flavour, he journeyed to their source in Zejiang, China, where he also discovered the oriental grapefruit, known locally as 'the forbidden fruit', a cross between Indonesian pomelo and Jamaican sweet orange.

Shed Distillery uses a combination of distillation methods: juniper, coriander seed, cardamom, angelica, orris root, star anise, caraway seed and meadowsweet are distilled on the pot still, while the gunpowder tea, lemon, oriental grapefruit and kaffir lime are vapour infused (page 28). For the perfect serve, add 40 ml of Drumshanbo Gunpowder Irish Gin to 140 ml of quality tonic with a wedge of fresh grapefruit and cubed ice. For a cocktail, try serving the gin with fresh lime and grapefruit juice, sugar syrup, fresh mint and grapefruit to make a Curious Jackalope.

Since the first edition of this guide, Shed Distillery now have distillery tours including tastings, a café and shop.

Micil Gin and Distillery

Galway, Co. Galway
Distillery and visitor centre

ESSENTIAL INFORMATION

Key botanicals (Micil Gin): juniper, heather, bog-myrtle, hawberry, Connemara bogbean

Output: not disclosed

Location: Oslo Bar, 226 Upper Salthill, Salthill, Galway, H91 N9WK

Telephone: 091 374 222

Email: info@micil.ie

Website: www.micildistillery.com

Facebook: www.facebook.com/micildistillery

Instagram: @micildistillery

Twitter: @micildistillery

Opening hours:
Monday-Sunday 0900-1700

Other reasons to go: Galway Cathedral, Galway City Museum, Eyre Square

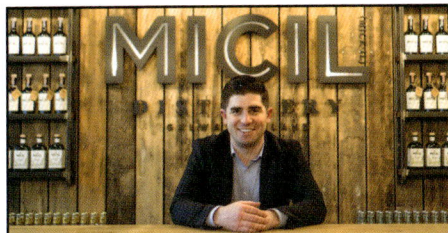

Pádraic Ó'Griallais developed a love for spirits from his grandfather, a fourth-generation distiller who began teaching him the craft from the age of 14. Pádraic's family specialized in poitín, a grape-based spirit similar to whisky which he calls the original Irish spirit. After a career in teaching, Pádraic decided to go back to his roots and opened Galway's first legal distillery for more than a hundred years, naming it after his great-great-grandfather Micil Mac Chearra, who began distilling in Connemara in 1848.

Pádraic saw there was a shared heritage between poitín and gin – they were both originally distilled from wine and botanicals – so decided to take a stab at gin. In July 2018, Micil Irish Gin was launched in tandem with the opening of the distillery's visitor centre. Pádraic makes the gin with botanicals picked from the Connemara coast and hedgerows and distils them using the one-shot method (page 28). He classifies the gin as a contemporary London Dry that's best served with a wedge of citrus and a quality tonic. For a cocktail, try it in a Connemara Collins or Micil Gin Sour.

Micil offers a distillery tour from 25 euros, where you learn about the history of whisky, poitín and gin, and how they're made. You also get to sample their gin and poitín – see website for booking information.

Listoke Gin, Distillery and Gin School

Drogheda, Co. Louth
Distillery and gin school

ESSENTIAL INFORMATION

Key botanicals (Listoke 1777 Gin): juniper, coriander seed, cardamom, cassia bark, orange, rowan berry, jasmine

Output: 40,000 bottles a year

Location: Unit 9 Tenure Business Park, Monasterboice, A92 Y3VF

Telephone: 00353 867958330

Email: hello@listokedistillery.ie

Website: www.listokedistillery.ie

Facebook: www.facebook.com/ listokedistillery

Instagram: @listokedistillery

Twitter: @listokedistill

Opening hours:
Tuesday-Friday 1000-1600
Saturday 1100-1600

Other reasons to go: Boyne Viaduct, Millmount Fort

Listoke Distillery & Gin School is a family-run company captained by the mother-daughter team Sarah and Bronagh Conlon (opposite, bottom right), with Bronagh's husband Sean as head distiller. Listoke Distillery was founded in 2016 and has since gone global with sales in Europe, the U.S., China, Australia and Singapore.

As the pride and joy of the distillery, Listoke 1777's flavour is robust and spicy. Sweet orange adds to the juniper's bitterness and the rowan berries' tartness, giving way to pleasant florals. The finish has an unexpected, spicy kick from the cardamom. You can enjoy Listoke 1777 neat, or as a Martini. The flavours are enhanced with the addition of an ice cube and a twist of orange peel, and of course it makes a terrific G&T.

Over the years, Listoke 1777 has won a number of prestigious awards such as the Best Gin in Europe, and two Gin Masters. Since launching this signature gin, Listoke Distillery have branched out and now produce a number of other exciting concoctions such as their Pink Cacao & Raspberry Gin, Chocolate Inferno Gin and Sloe Gin.

Listoke Distillery have also recently added other delicious spirits to their range, including Wise Owl Whisky. The recipient of two gold medals, Wise Owl is a blended Irish whisky finished in an imperial stout cast. It has a peaty undertone and a soft vanilla finish, has no added caramel or

sugar and is not chill filtered. The Listoke spirit family continues to grow with the addition of their brand new range of Blue Owl Vodka. It comes in three flavours – Original, Mixed Berry and Chocolate, which are great served with ice and your favourite mixer or in a cocktail.

The gin school (top) can not only claim to be the first gin school in Ireland, but is one of its best gintourism experiences. They do it properly: on arrival, you get a Listoke 1777 and tonic plus distiller-quality juniper berries and a twist of orange peel. Then a tour of the distillery, where you learn the brand's story.

Then back to the school where you are given three classic gin styles to taste – and are asked to work out which you prefer. Next, serious classwork: you explore botanicals in depth. You can then distil your own bottle of gin using a wide array of botanicals in individual mini-stills. While waiting for distillation to complete, you'll try some local food specialities and have more G&Ts to keep you going.

Sling Shot Gin and Lough Ree Distillery

Lanesborough, Co. Longford
Distillery

ESSENTIAL INFORMATION

Key botanicals (Sling Shot Gin): juniper, coriander seed, cardamom, citrus fruits, celery seed, mint, lemon balm, peat

Output: not disclosed

Location: Main Street, Lanesborough

Telephone: +35343 332 1542

Email: info@lrd.ie

Website: www.lrd.ie

Facebook: www.facebook.com/LoughReeDistillery

Instagram: @loughreedistill

Opening hours:
Monday-Friday 1000-1700

Other reasons to go: Rathcline Castle, St Mel's Cathedral, Inchcleraun Island

Three siblings are behind this operation – Peter and Michael Clancy and Sheila Mullen. Sheila worked in finance and hospitality while Peter was an engineer, and Michael a brewing consultant. Ally Alpine of the Celtic Whiskey Shop and Alan Wolstenholme, of the Scottish Distillers Association, are non-executive directors.

Slingshot Gin (bottom left) is Lough Ree's first product, possibly the first gin made in Co. Longford, launched in 2018 at their microdistillery. Four years later, whisky dominates their range, distilled in what claims to be Co. Longford's first modern distillery.

Sling Shot's most original feature (apart from the bright blue bottle) is its peat flavour. To achieve this, peat is distilled separately, as are citrus fruits (orange, pink grapefruit, lemon and lime) and fresh mint. The three distillates are then blended and added to the base gin spirit which is flavoured with the key botanicals listed above.

The result is a complex flavour, starting with a fresh citrus aroma, developing into a spicy boldness on the tongue and finishing with an earthy roundedness from the peat, plus a fresh waft of mint. It has won several international awards.

Sling Shot? The legendary Queen Maeve of Connaught was killed by a slingshot strike while bathing in Lough Ree. Lanesborough is on Lough Ree's northern tip.

Mór Irish Gin and Arderin Distillery

Tullamore, Co. Offaly

Distillery

ESSENTIAL INFORMATION

Key botanicals (Mór Irish Gin): juniper,
coriander, rosemary, blackberry,
raspberry, cranberry

Output: 60,000 bottles a year

Location: Unit 12 Cloncollig Industrial
Estate, Church Road, Tullamore, Offaly

Telephone: not disclosed

Email: info@arderindistillery.com

Website: www.moririshgin.com

Facebook: www.facebook.com/Moririshgin

Instagram: @moririshgin

Twitter: @MorIrishgin

Opening hours:
Monday-Sunday 0900-1600

Other reasons to go: Tullamore Drew
Visitors Centre, Clonmacnoise Abbey, The
Slieve Bloom Mountains

Eoin Bara, Arderin's founder and distiller, has an engagingly Irish attitude to life – and gin. He is a believer in the power of mantras, of good stories – and of bad decisions. The first two don't need explanation, but the last? In fact he doesn't mean real bad decisions, simply decisions that aren't entirely safe, such as when he decided to leave his steady job in a design agency and go into craft gin. A friend asked him after one too many gins "What do you love?" "I love gin" was his reply, only partly in jest.

Eoin gave in his notice and spent four months travelling the world learning how to make gin. Back in Ireland he started building the distillery in Tullamore, named after Arderin, the highest peak in the Slieve Bloom Mountains that rise from Ireland's central plain.

Mór (bottom left) is made in four stages: juniper, coriander, angelica and rosemary are distilled together; then the berries separately. Next all are blended together to achieve consistency and refine the taste and lastly the blend is distilled. The number of bottles produced varies. Eoin used to go to great lengths finding the purest water, driving into the mountains in a pickup truck and pumping fresh sandstone filtered mountain water into a tank, but gave up after the legality was questioned.

The first thing you notice about Mór is its beautiful berry-aroma on the nose. The taste on the tongue is earthy at first, with coriander and rosemary making a

big impression. Then it becomes sweet and juicy with bundles of fresh berry flavour at the core. The finish has a hint of pepper. He also produces Pineapple Edition Gin (previous page, top right).

The gin school, opened in 2019, in Donabate, North Dublin, left Arderin very much a working distillery.

Sliabh Liag Distillers

Ardara, Co. Donegal
Distillery

ESSENTIAL INFORMATION

Key botanicals (An Dúlamán Irish Maritime Gin): juniper, coriander, cassia bark, lemon peel, orange peel, carrageen moss, channel wrack, sweet kombu, dulse, pepper dulse

Output: 14,352 bottles a year

Location: Ardara Distillery, Woodhill, Ardara, Co. Donegal, F94 EH7X

Telephone: +353 74 954 1640

Email: tours@sliabhliagdistillers.com

Website: www.sliabhliagdistillers.com

Facebook: www.facebook.com/AnDulamanGin

Instagram: @andulamangin

Twitter: @andulamangin

Opening hours:
Booking advised for distillery tours
Monday-Saturday at 1000, 1200, 1400 and 1600

Other reasons to go: Sliabh Liag Cliffs, Maghera beach, Glencolmcille folk village, Ardara heritage town

With its signature savoury flavours, An Dúlamán Irish Maritime Gin has captured the *draíocht na farraige* (or the magic of the sea) and the attention of foodies and discerning gin drinkers alike. Distilling in Donegal since 2017, in the first legal still in the county for more than 175 years, Sliabh Liag Distillers have harnessed the flavour from seaweed to create a savoury gin that their distiller, Moira Doherty, describes as a love letter to the Donegal Coast.

Dúlamán is the Irish name for channel wrack, one of the five seaweeds used in the gin. The wild Atlantic coast of Donegal holds an extraordinary bounty for foragers, and their centuries-old knowledge of harvesting and of natural products is put to good use in a unique gin. Six conventional botanicals are used to create a robust base for the gin, brought together with five locally-harvested varieties of seaweed to capture the taste of the sea, and slowly distilled in a London Dry single shot process. Each batch yields less than 175 litres.

The gin is bottled at 43.2% ABV, allowing the delicate, complex flavours to be fully appreciated. Each tiny batch is bottled by hand with the batch numbers (linked to the lunar phases) and bottle numbers written on the neck label.

The taste starts with juniper, then reveals rich umami (savoury), brisk salt, buttery oyster, chestnut and tannin flavours. Given time, the finish moves from Turkish Delight to a comforting warmth.

An Dúlamán Gin is superb in a Negroni and works well with any premium tonic water, especially when garnished with grapefruit.

Gin Spotlight: Jim and Tonic at The Print House

In August 2022, Jim and Tonic took over residence at The Print House in Stratford, East London – their flagship venue.

Find them next to the canal on Sugar House Island, complete with onsite distillery, two bars, three kitchens, a coffee shop and outdoor seating. Their extensive range of gins are served from a converted double decker bus for a true London feel. It features an expanded food and drinks menu, various special events and entertainment, plus their brand new gin distillery, tasting room, off-trade store, and all-weather ping-pong table. The venue specializes in 'delicious gin, delicious food and delicious views' over East London. Open 8am to 11pm.

The Stratford location joins Jim's other London bars at Mercato Metropolitano in Elephant and Castle and Mercato Mayfair.

See page 66 for Jim and Tonic's full entry.

OTHER CRAFT GIN BARS AND DISTILLERIES

These bars and distilleries weren't quite right for the main section, but certainly deserve a mention.

Esker Spirits Gin and Distillery, Aboyne
Kincardine Estate, Kincardine O'Neil, Aboyne, Aberdeenshire, AB34 5AD
Founded in October 2015 by husband and wife team Steven and Lynne Duthie, Esker claims to be the first gin distillery in Royal Deeside, Aberdeenshire. Their main product, Esker Gin, is produced in copper stills, using more than 12 botanicals including silver birch sap. As we went to press they had a five gins on sale, and their latest release was a range of vodkas.

The Gin Vault, Birmingham
16 Gas Street, Birmingham, West Midlands, B1 2DS
This bar can be found in Birmingham's canal area and offers more than 350 gins, plus gin experiences. The Gin Experience includes a gin cocktail, a three-gin paddle (sample) board, plus tapas and dessert. They also offer a Gin Cocktail Masterclass, Afternoon G&T, and Bottomless Brunch.

The Escape Gin Bar, Brockenhurst
Thatched Cottage Hotel, 16 Brookley Road, Brockenhurst, SO42 7RR
Escape claims to be the New Forest's only specialist gin bar, offering more than 300 different gins, including locally made Conker (page 32), Pothecary (page 35-36) and Twisted Nose (page 84) gins. They offer Tasting Flights where you get three different gins to compare.

Cambridge Gin Laboratory, Cambridge
10 Green Street, Cambridge, CB2 3JU
The sister establishment of Cambridge Distillery, the Gin Laboratory has four rooms: the Classroom offers tastings and a history of gin production and you can also create your own gin recipe, if booked in advance; the Study is available for private hire; The Tasting Room offers a range of Cambridge Distillery Gins for sampling; and the Shop, where you can buy Cambridge Distillery products, and blend your own gin with no appointment necessary.

Gin and Juice, Cardiff

6 Castle Arcade, Cardiff, CF10 1BU
Gin and Juice, opened in December 2017, is a lively bar in Cardiff's city centre with an impressive and growing range of over 350 gins. Taking its inspiration from the Victorian arcades, the bar has a speakeasy vibe as well as a snug area. They offer breakfast, brunch, sharing boards, and a replete evening gin menu. Located in the Castle Quarter, you can lap up the atmosphere of central Cardiff.

The Wrecking Coast Gin and Distillery, Delabole

Pentire Workshops, Unit 2, High Street, Delabole, PL33 9BA
Avian Sandercock, Daniel Claughton, Steve Wharton and Craig Penn launched this distillery in 2014 after struggling to find a gin that ticked all their boxes. They wanted to capture Cornwall in a bottle and were determined to make a recipe using clotted cream. Avian steeps 12 of the botanicals in neutral grain spirit for two weeks before they are

added to the still and rested for seven days. He uses the vacuum distillation method to make a clotted cream and spirit mix, allowing it to stay cool so it isn't cooked and caramelized. This is then added to the still with the rest of the distillates before it's cut with Cornish natural spring water to 44%. They recommend serving the gin with a quality tonic, ice and a strawberry.

Celtic Whiskey Shop, Dublin
27-28 Dawson Street, Dublin 2
Don't be distracted by the name – this is Ireland's most important craft gin retail outlet alongside a similarly comprehensive Irish whisky selection. For enthusiasts, it is a must to visit when in Dublin. It's a well-organized, nicely presented shop, an Aladdin's cave for spirit nuts, opened by Ally Alpine in 2003. It hosts regular tastings, and also incorporates Wines on the Green, Dublin's specialist wine merchants. As we went to press the most expensive item on sale was Midleton Pearl Very Rare 30th Anniversary whisky at a whopping 11,000 euros a bottle, but with such a large stock there are items for all pockets. Another Ally Alpine venture is the Celtic Bar & Larder which he opened in Killarney in 2016.

Dublin City Gin, Dublin
Dublin, Ireland
Dublin City Gin launched in 2016, with a recipe created by partners who decided Dublin desperately needed its own gin. Founders Jim O'Connor, and Sheila Cooney. They use hand-picked rhubarb grown along the Grand Canal in Dublin, and their Irish milkspirit (derived from whey in cheese production) provides base of recipe. The gin now has over 30 accolades. They've since released a 100% Single Malt Whisky.

Bimber Gin and Distillery, Ealing
56 Sunbeam Road, London NW10 6JQ; info@bimber.co.uk
Darius Plazewski founded Bimber Distillery in 2015 with a focus on whisky. However, in 2016 they released Bimber Original Gin, which is dry with an earthy finish and notes of citrus and floral. They also produce London Classics, a sweeter gin, and in June 2019 they launched Da Hong Pao Tea Gin, made from organic oolong tea from China's Wuyi Mountain. All their gins are made with four times-distilled vodka infused with botanicals for 24

hours. They've since released Apogee XII, their new small batch pure malt whisky.

Mews Gin, East Horsley
East Horsley, Surrey, KT24 5DL
Father and son team Richard and Daniel Mew launched Mews Gin after two years of research and experimenting with different distillation methods and recipes. Their deadline was a family wedding in 2014, but they officially launched in 2015 after buying a 100-litre copper still called Betty. They use the vapour infusion method to distil 11 different botanicals, including lavender and pink peppercorns as the most prominent flavours. They recommend serving the gin with a quality tonic and a wedge of lime or a cucumber slice.

Silver Spear Gin, Fenagh
Smyth & O'Reilly Artisan Irish Distillers, Ballydarton House, Fenagh, Bagenalstown, County Carlow, Ireland
The microdistillery at Ballydarton House was founded by Smyth & O'Reilly Distillers in 2015 with the aim of producing artisan gin products. The building was home to John Henry Watson in the 1830s and the distillery's first product, Silver Spear Gin, was named after the award he received for skills in horsemanship against local militia in Colonial India. The gin is made with 13 different botanicals with a strong citrus and coriander flavour, and works well in a Gimlet.

Foxhole Gin, Haywards Heath
Bolney, Haywards Heath, RH17 5NB
Foxhole Spirits released their first gin, Foxhole Gin, in 2014. It's made using by-products of the English grape harvest, with which they make their own wine before it's distilled for two days to make a grape spirit. The result is then blended with neutral spirit and the botanicals: juniper, coriander, lemon zest, liquorice root, bitter orange, and grapefruit zest. The result is a smooth, aromatic gin which works well in a Dry Martini.

They also produce Hyke Gin, flavoured with botanicals inspired by the origins of the grapes used in the gin – Africa and South America – including coriander, myrrh, and rooibos.

Leeds Gin, Leeds
6 The Idas, Pontefract Road, Leeds, LS10 1SP
Leeds Gin Original is made with Leeds and Yorkshire's finest botanicals, in a traditional 35-litre copper pot still by distiller Sara Birkinshaw. Their first batch went on sale in March 2016. Sara sourced Yorkshire rhubarb from E. Oldroyd's in Leeds and freeze-dried it to preserve flavour so it can be enjoyed year-round. She spent many years looking for the perfect gin in bars of Palma, London and New York, and wanted to create a gin that represents Leeds to a T. It's best served with quality tonic and orange peel or in a Martini. Their delicious range can be bought from the online shop.

Lilliput Gin, Lilliput
Lilliput, Dorset
Andy Woodfield founded Lilliput Dorset Gin in 2017 hoping to capture the spirit of his hometown, Lilliput in Poole. The gin is based on the classic (and traditionally sweet) London Dry formula but rosemary, basil, thyme and olive give it a savoury dimension and a Mediterranean twist which Andy claims is in keeping with the nearby Jurassic coast. These botanicals are infused separately in a grain spirit before being blended with the rest, including hand-picked juniper from Bosnia. The mixture is then distilled in a copper still in small batches. Serve the gin with plenty of ice, a premium light tonic, rosemary, a wedge of lime and a Kalamata olive. As we went to press, they were preparing to reopen with new owners.

Sussex Hop Gin, Mayfield
Mayfield, East Sussex
James Rackham, founder of Emporia Brands and Mayfield Distilling Co., distils Sussex Hop Gin using seven botanicals plus Sussex hops. The botanicals are individually distilled then blended together in a 150-year-old copper pot still. The label depicts the local folklore of St Dunstan and the Devil: in the 10thC, Dunstan pulled the Devil by nose with blacksmith's tongs, after which the Devil flew off to cool down in the springs of Tunbridge

Wells, giving them a reddish hue. James also produces two gin liqueurs, both made with Sussex Hop Gin: Lucky Horseshoe Elderflower and Peach, made with fresh elderflower, peach, quince, lemongrass, and blackcurrant; and Cuckoo Line Rhubarb and Ginger, made with fresh rhubarb and ginger.

Elemental Cornish Gin, St Columb

Trewenna Barn, Tregonetha, Cornwall TR9 6EL
Husband and wife team Jonathan and Jilly Meyer founded the Elemental Cornish Gin Distillery in 2013. Having been inspired by the popularity of microdistilleries in London, they decided that Cornwall needed its own premium gin and Elemental Cornish Gin was launched a year later. Produced in batches of 200 bottles, it's made using the one-shot method in a traditional copper still. Twelve botanicals including juniper, coriander seed and cassia bark are steeped in organic neutral grain spirit overnight before distillation. The heads and tails are removed before the spirit is cut with Cornish spring water from Bodin Moor to 42%. They also produce Elemental Raspberry Gin, and Apple Gin. In 2018, Jon and Jilly received planning permission to build a larger distillery with a visitors' centre, offering distillery tours, tastings and other events. Everything would be run by solar power. To raise funds for the project, they launched a limited edition gin, Elemental Rising Tide, which they were offering as rewards to those who donated to the cause. In 2020 partners Nicki and Joe Woolley took the reigns of Elemental and are now the owners and faces of the brand.

Teasmith Gin, Udny

Udny, Aberdeenshire, info@teasmithspirits.com
Nick and Emma Smalley had always loved gin and were encouraged by the gin craze to make their own. They spent two years researching the industry, and developing their recipe before launching Teasmith Gin in 2015. It was inspired by the story of James Taylor, a 19thC tea planter from Aberdeenshire, who planted the first tea plantation in Sri Lanka – Teasmith Original centres around a Sri Lankan tea, Golden Tippy Orange Pekoe. They took it to Strathearn Distillery to perfect the recipe, which also includes juniper,

coriander, liquorice root, grains of paradise, orange peel, and honeyberry. All the botanicals, except the tea, are vapour infused. The tea is steeped in neutral grain spirit separately before it's blended with the rest of the botanicals, and left to rest for several days. It's then cut with water to 43%, producing around 600 bottles per batch. Nick and Emma recommend serving the gin with a quality tonic, plenty of ice and a sprig of mint.

In this index, craft gin bars and distilleries are arranged in alphabetical order by name.

INDEX

DUNCAN PETERSEN GUIDES

Charming Small Hotel Guides

Austria, Switzerland & The Alps

Britain & Ireland

France

Germany

Italy

Spain

On Foot Guides

Paris Walks

New York Walks

Venice Walks

Prague Walks

Rome Walks

Florence Walks

Boxed walking guides

Great Pub, Great Walk

Weekend Walks

Lake District Walks

London and the South East

Walker's Britain

Cycle Escapes London

Cyclist's Britain

Walker's Scotland

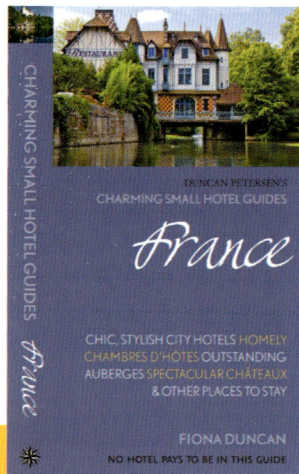

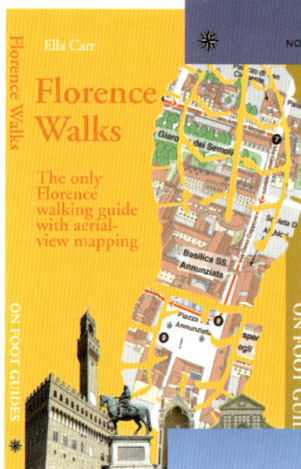

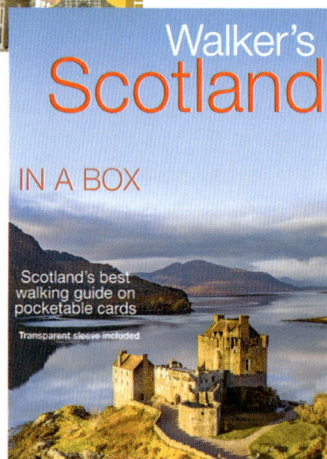

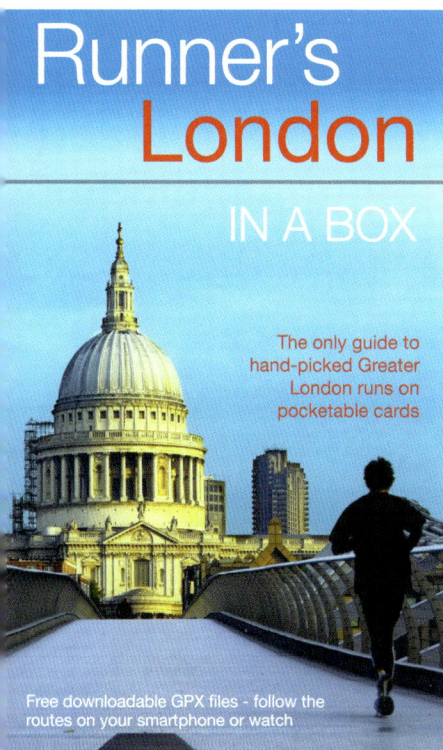
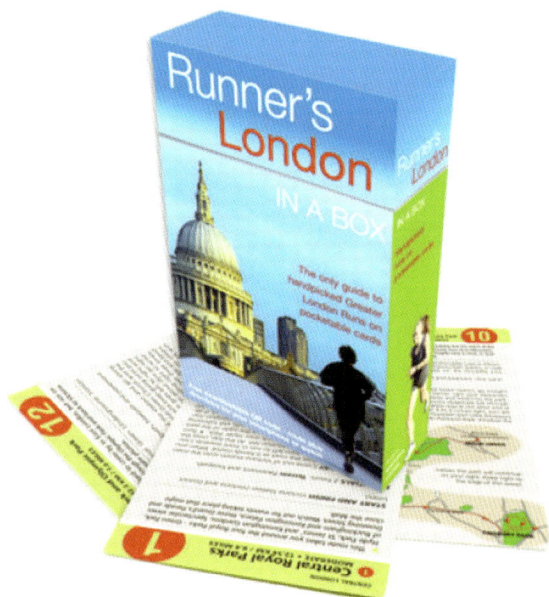

PICTURE CREDITS